Anonymous

Hygiene for young People

Adapted to Intermediate Classes and Common Schools

Anonymous

Hygiene for young People
Adapted to Intermediate Classes and Common Schools

ISBN/EAN: 9783337176778

Printed in Europe, USA, Canada, Australia, Japan

Cover: Foto ©ninafisch / pixelio.de

More available books at **www.hansebooks.com**

PATHFINDER PHYSIOLOGY No. 2

HYGIENE

YOUNG PEOPLE

INTERMEDIATE CLASSES AND COMMON SCHOOLS

A. S. BARNES & COMPANY
NEW YORK AND CHICAGO

PATHFINDER SERIES

OF TEXT BOOKS ON

ANATOMY, PHYSIOLOGY, AND HYGIENE.

With Special Reference to the Influence of Alcoholic Drinks and Narcotics on the Human System.

I.

FOR PRIMARY GRADES.

THE CHILD'S HEALTH PRIMER.

12mo. Cloth.

An introduction to the study of the science, suited to pupils of the ordinary third reader grade.

Full of lively description and embellished by many apt illustrations.

II.

FOR INTERMEDIATE CLASSES.

HYGIENE FOR YOUNG PEOPLE.

12mo. Cloth. Beautifully illustrated.

Suited to pupils able to read any fourth reader.

An admirable elementary treatise upon the subject.

The principles of the science more fully announced and illustrated.

III.

FOR HIGH SCHOOLS AND ACADEMIES.

HYGIENIC PHYSIOLOGY.

12mo. Beautifully illustrated.

A MORE ELABORATE TREATISE.

Prepared for the instruction of youth in the principles which underlie the preservation of health and the formation of correct physical habits.

Preface

* An Act relating to the Study of Physiology and Hygiene in the Public Schools.

"*The People of the State of New York, represented in Senate and Assembly, do enact as follows:*

"Section 1. Provision shall be made by the proper local school authorities for instructing all pupils in all schools supported by public money, or under State control, in physiology and hygiene, with special reference to the effects of alcoholic drinks, stimulants, and narcotics upon the human system."

Thus read, with slight modifications, the laws of four other states, viz., Vermont, Michigan, New Hampshire, and Rhode Island.

This book has been prepared to meet the demands of these states for intermediate grades of schools. Since the laws say that Physiology and Hygiene, with special reference to the effects of alcoholic drinks, etc., shall be studied by all pupils in the public schools, such of the obvious facts of Physiology as would render the Hygiene intelligible have been included.

Enough on the subject of Hygiene has been introduced to give a general knowledge of the laws of health; while, as the spirit and the letter of the laws direct, especial reference has been made to the effects of alcoholic drinks and other narcotics.

Eminent physicians and teachers have contributed helpful suggestions in the preparation of this work. Among the former are Prof. Palmer, M.D., LL.D., Dean of the Medical Department of Michigan University; Dr. Ezra M. Hunt, A.M., M.D., President of the section of the American Medical Association on State Medicine and Public Hygiene, Vice-President of the American Public Health Association, etc., and author of "Alcohol as a Food and Medicine."

Of the teachers who have helped in shaping these truths into a suitable form for young minds, first mention should be made of Miss Alice M. Guernsey, High School, Wareham, Mass.

The aid of Dr. Mary V. Lee, of the Oswego, N. Y., Normal School; Prof. Jones, Supt. of Public Instruction, Erie, Penn.; D. B. Hagar, Ph.D., Principal of the State Normal School, Salem, Mass.; Mr. E. P. Church, Supt. of Public Instruction, Greenville, Mich., and other practical instructors, is also gratefully recognized by the editor.

INTRODUCTION.

I have examined the manuscript of this book, and find it covering more matter that I think should be taught in the elementary lessons on life and health in the schools, than I have found in the other works, with similar objects, which I have had occasion to examine.

It is free from the errors which have been noticed and objected to in several other works on this subject designed for school use.

I also think it free from such overstatements as are likely to be produced by ardent zeal.

If all the facts contained in this little work are firmly lodged in the minds of the pupils in our public schools throughout the country, an immense work for good will be accomplished.

Being profoundly impressed with the enormous evils to our race produced by the habitual use of narcotics, including alcohol, opium, and tobacco, I can but rejoice at the promising efforts to make obligatory in the public schools the teaching of Physiology and Hygiene, with special reference to these narcotics, and I know of no work which is a better introduction to the subject than the present text-book.

Of the diseases, the degeneracy, the vices, and the general ill-being produced by the alcohol habit, all observers must be aware.

The evils of the opium habit are scarcely less, in proportion to its more limited extent, and the habit is, if possible, even less likely to be broken up when once established.

The tobacco habit, though less disastrous to individuals and in its moral and social effects upon communities, still, by its greater prevalence, is doing an amount of mischief, especially with boys, which none so fully know as those physicians who have given special attention to the subject.

The influence which indulgence in one narcotic has upon the resort to others, should be more fully recognized, and the great importance of abstinence from all of them will, by these teachings, it is hoped, be more fully understood and appreciated.

It therefore gives me great pleasure to say this much, and in this place, in favor of the objects and the execution of this work, and in commendation of the efforts of those who have had the labor of its preparation.

A. B. PALMER.

ANN ARBOR, Sept. 1, 1884.

TABLE OF CONTENTS.

CHAPTER	PAGE
Introduction	5
First Words	8
I.—Alcohol	9
II.—Fermentation	15
III.—Distillation	25
IV.—Tobacco	31
V.—Opium	37
VI.—Bones	41
VII.—Muscles	57
VIII.—Food	65
IX.—Are Narcotics Foods?	77
X.—Digestion	87
XI.—Respiration	109
XII.—Circulation	125
XIII.—The Skin	141
XIV.—Animal Heat	149
XV.—Alcohol and Life	157
XVI.—The Nervous System	165
XVII.—Special Senses	193
Index	203

FIRST WORDS.

"KNOW thyself," is old and good advice. As the body is an important part of a person, we are only obeying this counsel when we learn how it is built, how it lives, and what is good or bad for its health.

Because many people are ignorant of the true nature of alcoholic drinks and other poisons, the law in some parts of our country requires the pupils in the public schools to study the human body and the effects of these drugs upon it.

From these lessons you will learn, first, what these drugs are. That you may understand what they will do to those who use them, you must then learn about the human body and how to take care of it.

When you see what alcohol, tobacco, and opium, do to its many wonderful parts, and what trouble and sorrow they cause, you will know why it is dangerous to use them.

CHAPTER I.

ALCOHOL.

ALCOHOL is a colorless liquid with a stinging taste; it burns without soot, giving little light, but great heat. It is lighter than water, and can not be frozen.

It is used to dissolve gums, resins, and oils; to make smokeless flames; to take from leaves, roots, barks, and seeds, materials for making perfumes and medicines; and to keep dead bodies from decaying.

People do not usually drink clear alcohol (ăl′co hŏl). Rum, whiskey, wine, cider, gin, brandy, beer, etc., are water and alcohol with different flavors. Many million gallons of alcohol in these liquors are drunk every year by the people of this country.

ORIGIN OF ALCOHOL.

Water forms the larger part of grape, apple, and other fruit and plant juices. Green fruits contain much starch; as they ripen and become fit for food, this starch turns to sugar. Our sweet-tasting fruits and plants have sugar in their juices; and from such juices, boiled down, we get the sugar used for food.

If this fruit or plant juice is drawn off from its pulp, and then exposed to the open air at summer heat, the sweet part changes:. it is no longer sugar, because it has separated into a liquid called alcohol and a gas named car bon'ic ac'id.* Much of this gas goes off into the air; the alcohol remains in the liquid, changing a wholesome food into a dangerous drink.

ALCOHOL A POISON.†

A poison is any substance whose nature it is, when taken into the body, either in small or large quantities, to injure health or destroy life.

---

* A better, but less common name for this gas is carbonic dioxide.

† Dr. A. B. Palmer, of Michigan University, says: "Medical writers admit that by far the most disastrous and frequent cause of poisoning in all our communities, is the use of alcohol."

Dr. W. J. Youmans writes: "Alcohol . . . . a brain poison."

Proper food is wrought into our bodies; but poisons* are thrown out of them, if possible, because unfit to be used in making any of their parts.

In large doses, in its pure state, or when diluted, as in brandy, whiskey, rum, or gin, alcohol is often fatal to life. Deaths of men, women, and children from poisonous doses of this drug, are common.

In smaller quantities, or in the lighter liquors—beer, wine, and cider—when used as a beverage, it injures the health in proportion to the amount taken.

WHAT IS A NARCOTIC?

Any substance that deadens the brain and nerves is called a narcotic; for example, ether (e'thĕr) and chloroform (eḵlō'rō fôrm), which are given by the dentist, that he may extract

---

Dr. Alden, of Massachusetts, tells us: "On every organ they touch, alcoholic drinks act as a poison. There is no such thing as their temperate use. They are always an enemy to the human body. They produce weakness, not strength; sickness, not health; death, not life."

* Intoxicated means poisoned. The barbarians poisoned their arrows; hence, from the Latin *in*, into—and *toxicum*, a poison into which arrows were dipped, we get the word which describes the condition of a person under the influence of alcohol.

teeth without pain. Alcohol is taken for similar purposes, and is a powerful narcotic.

ALCOHOL AND WATER.

Into a bottle half full of water, pour alcohol to the top; then shake it well, being very careful not to spill any of the liquid. Now, the bottle is not full. The alcohol has mixed with the water, and it does this wherever it has a chance.

Oil and water will not unite; alcohol and water will always unite.

In our study of the human body, which is seven parts out of eight, water,* we shall see how alcohol, beginning at the lips, unites with the water in every part of the drinker's body which it reaches, thus robbing it of the needed liquid.

---

* I took one of those remains of the human body which have been preserved some thousands of years, and which is called an Egyptian mummy.

It was probably the body of one who had been a great priest or ruler; for it had been embalmed or preserved in the most expensive form of embalming and had been inclosed in a tomb which must have cost a small fortune.

I measured the mummy,—its length, its girth, and the relative size of its head and limbs and trunk. From these measurements I was able to estimate what would have been the weight of the

ALCOHOLIC APPETITE.

Like all narcotic poisons, alcohol has the fatal power of creating an increasing appetite for itself, that demands not only more frequent, but stronger and larger doses. The greater its work of ruin, the harder and more nearly impossible to overcome, will be its demand.

The appetite does not gain with equal rapidity upon all; but no one can tell how

---

body when its owner was moving on the earth in the midst of life and health. The weight of the body at that time, I reckoned, would have been 128 pounds.

In the condition of a mummy, in which it was now before me, nothing remained but the dried skeleton or bony framework, and the muscles and other organs completely dried. The body, in fact, had, in the course of ages, lost all its water.

In this state it weighed just sixteen pounds, and, as eight times sixteen are one hundred and twenty-eight, it is clear that seven parts out of eight of the whole body, or one hundred and twelve pounds, had passed away as water. In the remaining weight was included that of the skeleton, which contains but ten per cent. of water, and some mere remnants of canvas and pitchy substances, which had been used by the embalmers, and which, like the skeleton, still continued perfect.

The soft parts of this human body, by which all its active life, its moving and thinking functions, had been carried on, were, in fact, nearly all removed by the drying process, or loss of water, to which they had been subjected. They had not been destroyed by passing into new forms of matter, as occurs when a dead substance is allowed to decay in the open air; but they had completely lost the water which once gave them size, flexibility, shape, and capacity for motion.

Dr. B. W. Richardson, of London.

long he will be satisfied with a little. This craving, so easily formed, and so hard to overcome, clings to its victims. Sometimes after slumbering through years of abstinence (ăb'stĭ něnçe), it is wakened by the first taste.

The custom of putting wine and other alcoholic liquors into cooked foods, is a dangerous one, often causing the formation or return of a fearful appetite.

In this country, over 60,000 persons every year die as drunkards—that is, are killed by alcohol. None of them expected to become drunkards when they began to drink liquor; but they were ignorant, or careless, of the power of a little alcohol to create an appetite for more.

REVIEW QUESTIONS.

1. What is alcohol?—Name some of its qualities.
2. What are the uses of alcohol?
3. From what is alcohol made?
4. How can you prove that alcohol is a poison?
5. How many persons every year die as drunkards?
6. Under what names is alcohol drunk?
7. What is the difference between a food and a poison?
8. Describe Dr. Richardson's experiment with the mummy.
9. What is the effect of alcohol upon the water in the human body?
10. Why does the drinker of alcohol fail to realize his danger?

CHAPTER II.

FERMENTATION.

WHAT is fer men ta'tion? When moist animal or vegetable matters are exposed to warm air, certain changes which take place alter their nature; these changes are produced by a process called fermentation.

When sugar is turning to alcohol and car bon'ic ac'id, the latter escapes in little bubbles, giving the entire liquid the appearance of boiling. We call this process, and others much like it, fermentation, from a Latin word which means to boil.

There are several kinds of fermentation. In these lessons we shall learn about only two of them.

I. *Vi'nous Fermentation*—the change of sugar to alcohol and carbonic acid.

II. *A ce'tous Fermentation*—the change of alcohol and other substances to vinegar.

VINOUS FERMENTATION.
BACTERIA AND YEAST.

If you should look at a drop of stagnant water under a strong mi′cro scope, you would be quite likely to find it full of small living things, so tiny that you could not see them at all with the naked eye; these mi nute′ animal and vegetable forms are alive, and often in rapid motion.

In the air, also, are many living forms, too small to be seen by the naked eye, called bacteria (băc tē′ rĭ á).

There are particles coming from them much smaller than the full-grown bacteria, which will become bacteria by growth. These are called spores, and are floating almost every-where in the air, and, from their extreme smallness, can get into places where the bacteria might not be able to come.

They have been carefully studied with the help of the microscope, and we know that, instead of the air, it is these bacteria or their spores in the air, which produce fermentation in certain liquids.

The juices of the grape, apple, and many other fruits, will, if placed under the right conditions, ferment by the action of these living forms.

In order to ferment some other liquids and thus obtain intoxicating drinks, yeast* must be added. In this way some people brew home-made beer—by steeping various roots, barks, and herbs in water, and adding yeast and sugar enough to cause fermentation. The alcohol that is formed by the change of the sugar, makes the beer a dangerous drink.

When a liquid is fermenting, the little bubbles of carbonic acid carry a froth to the top, which can be used as yeast to act on other liquids. At the bottom lie the "settlings," a half-solid mass, sometimes called the lees. Between the froth and the lees is a thin, intoxicating liquid, which people drink under different names, as, wine, cider, beer, etc.

Dry sugar will not ferment, nor will alcohol be formed in liquids which have an

---

* Yeast is really a plant, and it is the growth of the yeast plant which causes fermentation in these liquids.

excess of sugar. The united action of sugar, water, heat, and of the bacteria or spores in the air, or of yeast—each in the right proportion—are always required to produce alcohol.

ALCOHOL FROM GRAINS.

Starch forms a large part of rye, corn, barley, and other grains. If these are kept moist and warm—as when planted in the earth in spring or summer,—their starch turns to sugar, when the grain, which is a seed, begins to grow. Chew a grain of sprouted corn or barley, and you will find it sweet.

Barley is kept moist with water until it sprouts, or throws out little roots. During this process, most of the starch that is in the barley, changes to sugar. Heat is then applied, strong enough to dry out all the moisture of the barley and kill the young roots.

Grain thus treated is called malt, and from this malt, pale ales and beers are made.

Heating to a higher temperature, so as slightly to burn the sprouted grain, makes dark malt, from which porter and stout—dark colored drinks—are manufactured.

If the sugar thus formed in barley is dissolved out of the grain with water, and yeast is added, and the whole exposed to warm air, another change takes place,—the sugar which was once starch, becomes alcohol, and carbonic acid. By this process, a good food has been changed to a poison; for the barley has become an intoxicating drink—ale, beer, or porter.

ALCOHOL AND BREAD.

We must not conclude that fermentation is never a good thing. If it is stopped at just the right point, and the alcohol all driven off by heat, it improves some kinds of food.

Crushed grain, or flour, is a valuable food; but, in this form, is not pleasant to eat. Yeast added to warm, moistened flour causes fermentation. A little sugar in the flour itself (called free sugar) will turn to alcohol and carbonic acid gas. This gas, in a thin liquid, would pass off into the air. But it is imprisoned by the sticky dough, and puffs it up with little cells in its effort to escape, thus making the otherwise solid mass, light and spongy.

The small quantity of alcohol which was formed, largely evaporates, and the gas escapes when the dough is placed in the strong heat of the oven; a light, sweet loaf of bread is left, that is better food than the flour.

Alcohol turns to vapor with less heat than water. In bread baked enough to be food fit for the human stomach, the alcohol has been turned to vapor by the heat of the oven, and has passed off into the air.

People who are ignorant of the truths you are learning in these lessons, have supposed that because fermented dough makes good bread to eat, therefore fermented barley-juice must make good beer to drink. But you know the alcohol stays in the beer and not in the bread, and that simple fact makes the difference, in this case, between a food and a poison.

AMOUNT OF ALCOHOL IN FERMENTED LIQUORS.

In one hundred parts of the fermented juice of apples, or cider, there are from two to ten parts of alcohol. In one hundred parts of beer—the fermented juice of barley—there are from three to ten parts of alcohol.

In one hundred parts of the fermented juice of grapes and other kinds of fruit, or wines, there are from twelve to thirty-seven parts of alcohol (or six to seventeen, by weight).

It is estimated (in 1880) that twenty-two and three-quarter million gallons of alcohol are consumed every year by the people of this country, in beer alone.

This makes nearly one-half gallon of pure alcohol used by every man, woman, and child of our 50,000,000—if all were foolish enough to drink it.

As very many people drink no beer at all, some of the beer-drinkers must get more than this one-half gallon of poison during each year. Further study will show you the consequences of the use of this great quantity of alcohol.

HEAT AND FERMENTED LIQUORS.

If you were to place fermented liquors of any kind in an open kettle over strong heat, their charm for the wine, cider, or beer-lover, would soon be gone. It is for the sake of the alcohol they contain, that people are fond of these drinks, and this passes away in the form of vapor from the boiling liquid; the liquid which is left, has an insipid taste, and no one would care to drink it.

ALCOHOL IN NATURE.

It is a mistake to suppose that because grapes, apples, and barley, are healthful foods, that wine, cider, and beer, made from them, must also be healthful.

It is important to remember that fermentation entirely changes the character of the substance it works upon. Nature rots her various plant forms; but while the juice remains protected from the air by the skin or husk of the unbroken grain, plant, or fruit, its sugar will not ferment—therefore, alcohol is never found in them.

ACETOUS FERMENTATION.

ALCOHOL AND VINEGAR.

All vegetable substances come from earth, air, and water, and return to them again.

Through the process of fermentation, vegetable liquids go back to earth, air, and water. After the alcohol is formed, if it remains in the vegetable juice, exposed to moderately warm air, the second kind, or acetous fermentation, takes place, changing the alcohol to a sharp acid, called acetic acid and commonly known as vinegar.

When the cook has not baked the bread at just the right time—that is, has not stopped the fermentation before acid began to form in the dough, we say "the bread is sour". This acid does not pass off in the heat of the oven as alcohol does, but remaining gives a sour taste to the bread.

Acetic acid is as different from alcohol, as alcohol is from sugar. It is used for food. Vinegar is made in this way from hard cider and other fermented liquors, and will change, in its turn, if left in the same conditions that produced it, and lose its acid taste; its water all evaporating, nothing will remain but a brown powder.

The earth, air, and water have claimed again the matter only loaned to make the fruit, plant, or grain.

REVIEW QUESTIONS.

1. What is fermentation?
2. Why do fermenting liquids appear to be boiling?
3. What kinds of fermentation shall we consider?
4. If you look through a strong microscope at stagnant water, what would you see?
5. What are bacteria?
6. What are spores? and where found?
7. What produces fermentation in fruit juices?
8. How are some other liquids made into intoxicating drinks?
9. Why are home-made beers dangerous drinks?
10. What causes froth at the top of a fermenting liquor? and how is it used?
11. What is there between the froth and the lees?
12. What is necessary to produce alcohol?
13. What forms the chief part of grain?
14. How is this starch changed? Prove this.
15. How is the starch in barley turned to sugar?
16. What is malt? and what is made from it?
17. How does alcohol get into the beer?
18. How can fermentation be made to improve some foods?
19. What takes place when yeast is added to warm, moistened flour?
20. What makes bread light and spongy?
21. What becomes of this alcohol and carbonic acid gas in the dough? In beer, wine, and cider? (See other questions on p. 36.)

CHAPTER III.

DISTILLATION.

WHEN a liquid is changed to a vapor by heat, and that vapor is turned again to a liquid by cold, the process is called distillation (dĭs tĭl lā′tion).

Cold surfaces condense the moisture in the night air, and we say: "The dew is falling." By the heat of the sun, these drops of water are turned again to vapor that rises and spreads itself in the air; this is again changed to water by cold, and falls in the form of dew or rain. Thus, with her own heat and cold, "Nature is ever distilling."

Unless sugar is dissolved in water, it will not turn to alcohol; therefore, when first formed, alcohol is always mixed with water.

Alcohol and water could not be separated, until men, in imitation of nature, learned to distill.

Every child who has watched the steam

puffing from a tea-kettle, knows that heat will turn a liquid to vapor. Some liquids require less heat than others for this change. When two such liquids are mixed, one can be made to pass off in vapor, leaving the other. Thus alcohol and water may be separated.

Put a fermented liquor into a kettle over the fire, with a pipe in its closely-fitting spout to carry off the steam. Nearly all the alcohol will pass off in vapor before the water comes to the boiling point.

If this pipe is of the right length and is cooled by ice or cold water, the vapor, while passing through it, will turn to a liquid and drip from the end of the pipe. If you apply a lighted match to this new liquid, it will burn with a pale blue flame, giving out intense heat.

It is mainly alcohol which has been separated—distilled—from the fermented mixture. What remains in the kettle is principally water. The alcohol is unchanged in its nature; but is stronger, because not so much diluted with water.

DISTILLATION. 27

Fig. 2.

Experiment.—You may easily make this experiment for yourselves.

Put some hard cider into a teapot (*b*), and fasten a piece of rubber tubing (*e*) about two feet long to the spout.

Let the other end of the tubing reach into a bottle (*d*) standing in a pail of cold water or on a block of ice (*c*).

Heat the cider by means of the lamp (*a*), being careful not to make it hot enough for the water in the cider to boil.

If the cider is not very strong, you may have to re-distill it before you find the alcohol is pure enough to burn.

DISTILLED LIQUORS.

In the manner just described, brandy is distilled from wine or cider; rum from fermented molasses; whiskey from fermented corn, barley, or potatoes; gin from fermented barley, or rye, afterward distilled with juniper berries. Ordinarily these distilled liquors are about one-half pure alcohol.

Some of the water passes over with the alcohol, so that these liquors are often distilled a second, and even a third time, to make them stronger of alcohol.

The alcohol usually sold is distilled from fermented molasses; but it can be made from any fermented liquor. It is so greedy for water that entirely pure alcohol can be produced only by distilling it with some substance such as lime, that is still more eager for water, and will take it from the alcohol.

DRUGGED LIQUORS.

Wine in its many forms was probably the first, and, for many centuries, the only known intoxicating drink.

The ancients supposed that each of the various fruit juices made a different kind of liquor; but you see all of them are mainly alcohol and water. The different taste of each, if it is really what it claims to be, is due to its own peculiar fruit, grain, or plant flavor.

Poisonous drugs and coloring matter are often added to alcohol and water to imitate the various liquors. So much of this is done that many of the fermented and distilled liquors now sold and used, contain other poisons added to their own ever-present one —alcohol. As this is the most dangerous of all, the idea that "unadulterated whiskey" or the "pure, fermented juice of the grape," can be "good," is a mistake.

HOW ALCOHOL WAS DISCOVERED.

The people who lived about 700 years ago, thought that somewhere, if they could only find them, were two things that would greatly bless the world. First, something that would turn iron and all common metals into gold, and thus easily and greatly enrich the finder;

second, an "elixir of life," which would prevent sickness and death, and keep those who drank it forever young.

The men who tried many curious experiments in search of these two wonders, were called alchemists (ăl'kĕ mĭsts). It is supposed an Arab, named Albucasis, was thus led to discover alcohol by distilling it from wine.

His career of intoxication and violence was short. He had found not the "elixir of life," but the "water of death."

REVIEW QUESTIONS.

1. What is distillation?
2. Show that "Nature is ever distilling."
3. Describe the process of distillation of liquors.
4. Why are they distilled?
5. What are the principal distilled liquors?
6. From what is each made?
7. How is pure alcohol obtained?
8. What two substances form the greater part of all liquors?
9. How are the different plant flavors imitated?
10. Are "pure fermented liquors" healthful and safe? Why?
11. What led to the discovery of alcohol?
12. How did it affect its discoverer?

CHAPTER IV.

TOBACCO.

UNTIL within a few years, the Middle and part of the Southern States have been the chief tobacco-raising regions of our country. Now, however, the cultivation of tobacco has spread, until many fertile valleys, even as far north as Canada, are devoted to the growth of "the weed."

The plant reaches a height of several feet, and has large, spreading, pale-green leaves, which are dried, and then made into cigars or prepared to be smoked in pipes, or chewed, or used as snuff.

NICOTINE.

Tobacco, a powerful narcotic, contains a substance called nicotine (nĭc'o tĭne). A single drop, if put on the tongue of a dog, will soon kill the animal. An ordinary cigar contains nicotine enough to kill two men, if taken pure.

One has to learn to like tobacco. Boys who try it, know that at first it gives them headache, dizziness, and sickness at the stomach. Their poor bodies try to tell them they are taking a poison.

If they keep on, the nicotine deadens their nerves, so they do not feel these effects, though they are more or less injured all the time.

CIGARETTES.

Many boys and young men learn to smoke by beginning with cig ar ettes'. These seem harmless because they are so small; but they are one of the worst possible preparations of tobacco.

The smoke of the paper wrappings is irritating to the lungs, and the cigarettes send more poisonous fumes into the delicate air-cells, than a pipe or a cigar would do.

Drinking men are almost always smokers or chewers, and many a drunkard owes his ruined life and happiness, to the appetite for narcotics formed by the use of tobacco, and the company into which it led him.

Old cigar-stumps are often picked up from the streets and smoked or made into cigarettes. This is worse than disgusting; for, in this way, diseases may be spread, coming from the mouths of the first users. These stumps are the "strongest" part of the cigars—that is, they contain the most nicotine, which thus goes into the cigarettes.

TOBACCO AND GROWTH.

A boy who uses tobacco runs the risk of being dwarfed in body, mind, and soul;—of becoming a nervous, sickly man, with a weak memory and a feeble heart.

Physicians agree that many and serious troubles result from its use, even by adults;—it is certain that growing boys can never indulge in it with safety.

An eminent physician—Dean of one of the leading medical colleges in this country—(Dr. A. B. Palmer, of the University of Michigan), says that young men who learn to smoke or chew tobacco, destroy on an average, by so doing, one-fifth of the enjoyment and value, and at least one-tenth of the length of their lives.

As with other narcotics, using a little makes one long for more; the boy who begins with one or two cigars a day, soon increases the number.

Many men who are now slaves to this poison, would gladly be free from it; and very few tobacco-users would advise their sons to adopt the expensive, uncleanly, and worse than useless habit.

COST OF TOBACCO AND ALCOHOL.

What is the yearly expense of a five-cent mug of beer for each week-day, and two on Sundays? How many barrels of flour would this money buy at $6.00 a barrel?

What is the annual cost of the habit to a boy who spends five cents for cigarettes each day of the year? If, instead of burning it up, the boy, when fourteen years old, puts the value of the cigarettes into the Savings-Bank daily, what will it amount to by the time he is twenty-one?

If a man earns one dollar a day, and spends daily five cents for tobacco and five cents for beer, what part of his earnings is thus worse than wasted on these narcotics?

If twenty cents a day be spent for cigarettes and beer, what amount will be lost to the user in three months' time?

What amount would be saved in ten years' time, if a man who spends thirty cents a day for liquor, should give up the habit entirely?

How much will the expense of "treating" be likely to increase the amount one spends for alcohol and tobacco?

REVIEW QUESTIONS.

1. In what sections of this country is tobacco raised? Describe the plant.
2. Give proof of the poisoning power of nicotine.
3. What are the usual effects when one uses tobacco for the first time?
4. Why does the tobacco-user not continue to feel these effects?
5. Why are cigarettes especially harmful?
6. How may the use of tobacco be the means of leading one to drink liquors?
7. What risks does a boy run in using tobacco?
8. How does the appetite for tobacco change with the use of the drug? Why?
9. Which is the more profitable purchase—tobacco or flour? Why?

CHAPTER II.

1. Describe the appearance of a fermenting liquid.
2. What conditions will prevent the formation of alcohol from sugar?
3. What is the effect of heat on fermented liquors?
4. How much alcohol is there in beer? In cider? In wine?
5. How much alcohol is drank in beer in one year in this country?
6. How much would this make for one person?
7. What effect has boiling on fermented drinks?
8. How is the character of a substance affected by fermentation?
9. Describe acetous fermentation.
10. Why is bread sometimes sour?
11. Contrast acetous acid with alcohol. For what is it used? To what will it turn?

CHAPTER V.

OPIUM.

THE white poppy is a plant which is largely cultivated in India and China. If little slits are cut in the unripe seed-vessels, drops of milky juice come out. When dry, these are carefully scraped off and sold as opium (ŏ′pĭ ŭm).

From this opium, are made laudanum (lạu̇′da nŭm), morphine (môr′phĭne), paregoric (păr e gŏr′ic), and the various kinds of soothing-syrups. It is one of the most deadly of the narcotic poisons.

EFFECTS.

Usually, these various forms of opium are taken at first by the advice of the doctor, to relieve pain. But the appetite, like that for alcohol and tobacco, grows stronger, and the dose is made larger, as the habit gains upon its victim.

Opium does not make one violent, so as

to injure and murder others, as alcohol often does; but its effects on the users themselves are, if possible, even worse than those of alcohol.

At first, the user seems to be in a pleasant and wonderful dream; then he grows stupid and unconscious. When he comes to his senses again, there is a feeling of horror; to free himself from this, he longs for more of the drug, and will get it if possible. He seems to lose all power of self-control, and breaks the most solemn promises, if, by doing so, he can obtain the poison.

Many lives that might have been grand and noble, have been destroyed by opium. Druggists often have regular opium-customers: of these, there are many more women than men, because women are more subject to nervous diseases, and hence are more likely to learn to use this drug.

Those who have the care of children, frequently quiet them by the use of soothing-syrup. It stops the baby's cry, of course; but it does it by deadening the nerves and poisoning the tender child-life, often leaving injuries from which it never recovers. An overdose at once kills the little one.

Gin and other liquors are sometimes used for the same purpose. Because this practice injures the health and often creates a craving for alcohol, it is a cruel betrayal of trust on the part of those charged with the care of helpless infants.

THE NARCOTIC HABIT.

Chloral (klō′ral) and chloroform (klō′ro fôrm) are often used in sickness; but, like opium, are narcotics, and therefore dangerous helps. They should never be used in health, or on trivial occasions, or for any length of time.

One narcotic is very likely to lead to another. A gentleman once tried to break off the habit of smoking, by drinking wine instead. He found the wine was enslaving him; he tried morphine, and soon became its victim. At last, with a body sadly wrecked, he returned to tobacco, his first enemy, with his naturally fine abilities ruined through the appetite for narcotics.

Turning from one narcotic to another is merely a change of masters. The only hope for the poor victim lies in his power to stop using all of these poisons.

REVIEW QUESTIONS.

1. How is opium obtained?
2. Under what names is it sold?
3. Describe its effects on the user.
4. Why are there more opium-users among women than among men?
5. Why does soothing-syrup stop a child's cry?
6. What other narcotics are used in a similar way?
7. Is it safe and right to so use them? Why?
8. Why are opium, chloral, and chloroform called narcotics?
9. Is any thing gained by changing one narcotic for another?
10. What is the only safe rule in regard to the use of these poisons?

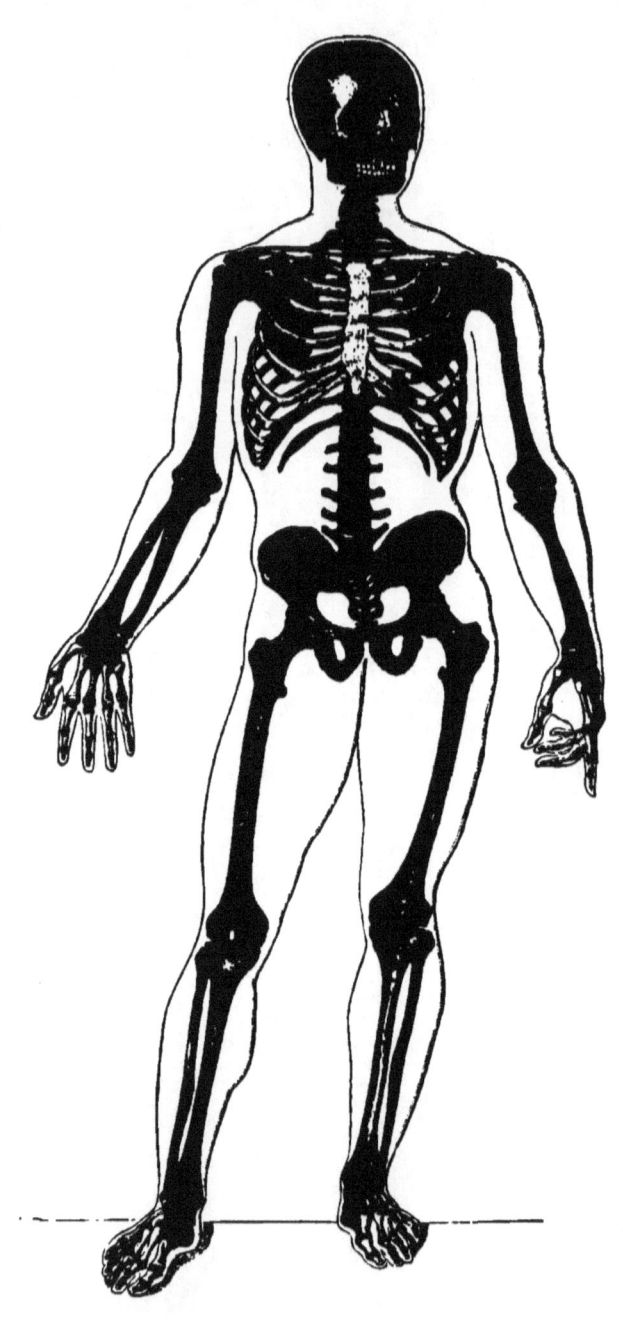

CHAPTER VI.

BONES.

ANY part of an animal or vegetable body which has some special work to do, is called an organ. For example, the root takes up food for the plant; the eye is the organ of sight; the nose is the organ of smell.

Plants and animals are called organic bodies, because they have organs. Stone, iron, coal, and other minerals, are called inorganic bodies, because they have no organs.

The solid parts of the body are called tissues; thus we speak of the fatty-tissue, and the muscular-tissue.

THE HUMAN SKELETON.

This is so much like the skeleton of the ox or the cat, that studying their bones will help us to understand about our own.

BONES.

The human skeleton is composed of about two hundred separate bones. It forms the frame-work of the body, and furnishes a hard surface to which to fasten the flesh. It also protects the softer parts within, as the heart and lungs.

Fig. 4.

The thigh-bone (femur) sawed lengthwise.

SHAPE OF THE BONES.

Some are long, like those of the leg and arm; some are flat, like the bones of the head. In the ankle and wrist, they are short and irregular. All are shaped for their special uses in the body.

COMPOSITION OF THE BONES.

The bones are made of both mineral and animal matter.

To prove this, burn the leg-bone of a chicken in a slow fire; the animal matter will pass away, leaving a white substance the shape of the bone, until it is roughly touched —then it crumbles into dust. This is a kind of lime, and is valuable as a fertilizer.

The mineral matter may be removed by soaking a bone for a few hours in weak muriatic acid; the animal matter, or gristle, which is left, is soft and yielding, so that you may bend the bone, or tie it in a knot if long enough.

Egg-shells, also, contain lime. You may easily puzzle some of your friends, by putting an egg into a very small-necked bottle. All that you need to do is to soak the egg in weak acid, until the shell is so soft that it can be pushed through the neck of the bottle; once in, it will take its natural form again.

In childhood, the bones contain more animal than mineral matter, and so are not easily broken; in old age, there is more mineral than animal matter, and the bones are brittle and break very easily.

GROWTH OF THE BONES.

Like the rest of the body, the bones are fed by the food we eat.

Mix some bright coloring-matter that is not poisonous, as madder, with the food given to a young pig for a time, and then give the same food without the color. If the animal be killed after a short time, each bone will show the color of the madder. This proves that the bones were made from the food the animal had eaten.

LIFE OF THE BONES.

In infancy, bones begin their life as a sort of jelly, which hardens into gristle, or cartilage, as the child grows. This cartilage receives from the blood several kinds of food, the most important of which are certain forms of lime; these, little by little, change the soft gristle to hard bone.

Farmers give their hens oyster-shells, which contain lime, so that they may have material for the shells of the eggs they lay. Human beings get lime from milk and other foods containing it. When the bones have too little lime, they are soft and weak.

A fatty matter, called marrow, is in the inside of the long bones, with blood-vessels passing through it and through very small holes in the bone itself, carrying food for its life and growth. Covering each bone is a very thin, tough skin.

BROKEN BONES.

If an iron rod in a steam-engine should break, would it be enough to fasten the broken pieces tightly, end to end, and then wait a few weeks for the iron to grow together? You laugh at the idea. But the bones do that—they mend themselves when broken.

All that is needed is to put the ends in place and fasten them tightly with splints and bandages, so that they can not move. Soon a jelly-like substance, made from the blood in the bone, connects the two ends; then this changes to gristle, and, by-and-by, into solid bone, and the break is mended.

The bones of young people, when broken, unite readily, and, in a few weeks, become as strong as ever. This is due both to the composition of the bones and the abundant supply of repairing substances in the blood.

A bone broken late in life is a long time in being united, and is likely to remain weak.

THE SKULL AND FACE BONES.

These protect the organs of sight, hearing, smell, and taste, and the brain, the organ of thought.

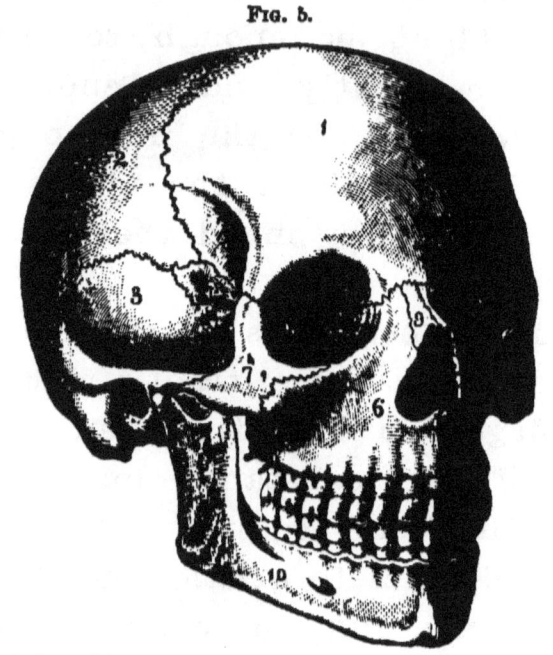

Fig. 5.

The skull.—1, *frontal bone;* 2, *parietal bone;* 3, *temporal bone;* 6, *superior maxillary (upper jaw) bone;* 7, *malar bone;* 9, *nasal bone;* 10, *inferior maxillary (lower jaw) bone.*

THE TRUNK.

The bones of the trunk are the backbone, or spine, the ribs, the breast-bone, and the hip bones. The spine is composed of a series of twenty-four little bones, called vertebræ.

THE TRUNK. 47

Cushions of gristle lie between the vertebræ. If it were not for this, walking and running would jar the body greatly.

In sitting or standing, as we do through the day, these cushions are pressed, and so flattened. When we lie down at night, they return to their natural shape, much as a rubber eraser would do if you pressed it with your finger and then took the finger away. For this reason, one is really a little taller in the morning than at night.

The ribs are slender, curved bones, twenty-four in number, twelve on each side of the body. Behind, they are attached to the backbone; in front, seven pairs are joined to a dagger-shaped bone, called the breast-bone; three pairs are joined by gristle to each other, and then to the breast-bone; two pairs are "floating" ribs. (See Fig. 7.)

FIG. 6.

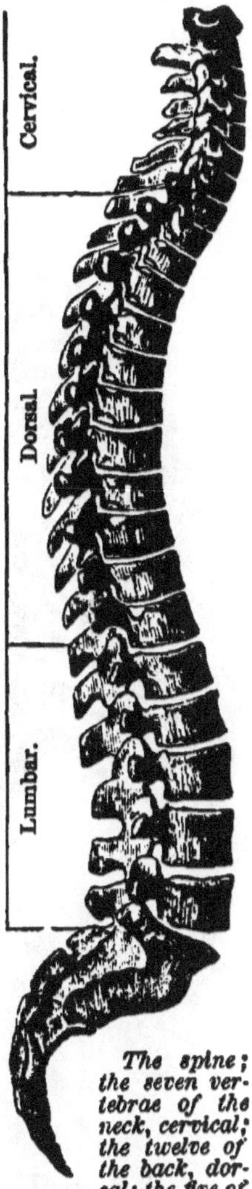

The spine; the seven vertebræ of the neck, cervical; the twelve of the back, dorsal; the five of the loins, lumbar.

The hip bones are two large, irregular bones which form the side walls of the lower part of the trunk.

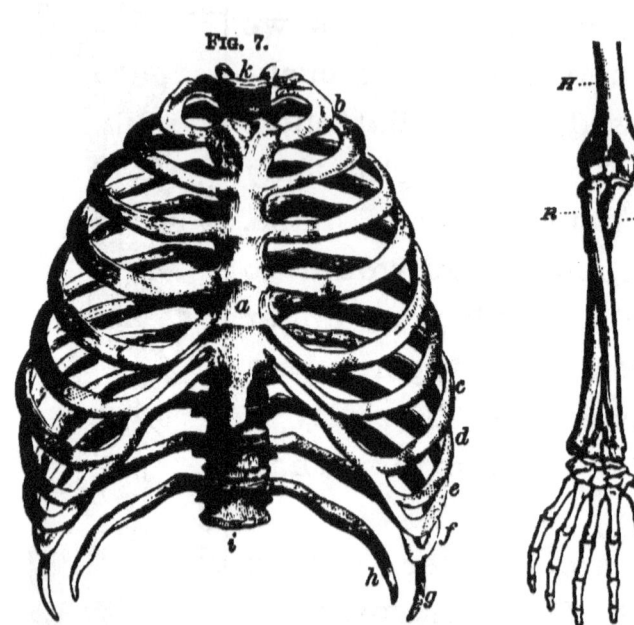

The chest; a, the sternum or breast-bone; b to c, the true ribs; d to f, the false ribs; g, h, the floating ribs; i to k, the dorsal vertebrae.

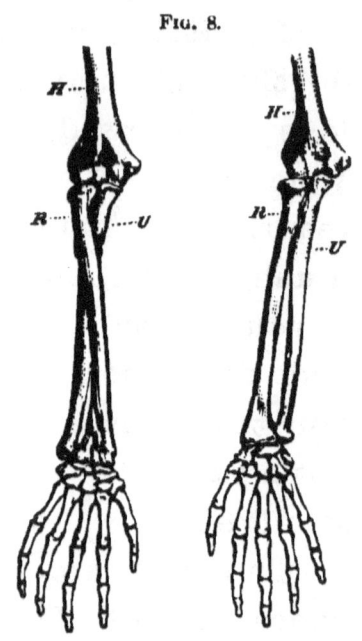

Bones of right fore-arm; H, the humerus; R, the radius; U, the ulna.

THE UPPER LIMBS.

The collar-bones are in front of the upper part of the body; the shoulder-blades, at the back. Fastened to the latter, on each side, is the large bone of the upper arm; below the elbow, are the two bones of the fore-arm, and those of the wrist, the palm of the hand, and the thumb and fingers.

Fig. 9.

Bones of the foot; a, b, c, d, e, f, g, *bones of the ankle and instep;* h, i, *forward part of the foot;* k, l, *bones of the great toe;* m, n, o, *bones of the other toes.*

Fig. 10.

The shoulder-joint; a, *the collar-bone;* b, *the shoulder-blade;* c, *the large bone of the upper arm.*

THE LOWER LIMBS.

The thigh-bone, in the leg above the knee, joins the hip bone. Below the knee are the two bones of the lower leg and those of the ankle, foot, and toes. In front of the knee-joint is a small bone, called the knee-pan.

As there are nineteen bones in each hand or foot, they have a great variety of motions. A hand or foot made of one bone, would be stiff and clumsy.*

CAVITIES.

There are two principal cavities, or hollow places, in the bony frame-work.

The first is the cavity of the head. The second is a great hollow place, extending from the neck to the legs, divided into two parts by a partition called the diaphragm (dī'a frăm).

In the upper part—the chest—are the heart and lungs; in the lower—the abdomen—are the liver, stomach, bowels or intestines, kidneys, and other organs.

---

* Many Japanese and Chinese use their toes almost as readily as they do their fingers. They will pick up tools with their toes and work with them, while managing other instruments in their hands.

Workmen in Constantinople always sit on the ground, even in planing a board; sometimes they hold a long-handled chisel in the left hand, "while the toes guide the cutting edge in turning beautiful forms in a lathe."

"Arabs braid ropes with their toes and fingers laboring in concert." Our toes are so cramped in their stiff leather boots that we do not pretend to use them.

TABLE OF THE PRINCIPAL BONES.
THE HEAD AND FACE.

No.	Scientific Name.	Common Name or Position.
1.	Frŏnt'al	Forehead.
1.	Oc çĭp'i tal	Back of the head.
2.	Pa rī'e tal	Upper side walls of the head.
2.	Tĕm'po ral	Lower side walls of the head.
2.	Su pē'ri or Măx'il la ry	Upper jaw.
1.	In fē'ri or Măx'il la ry	Lower jaw.
2.	Mā'lar	Cheek.
2.	Nā'ṣal	Nose.

THE SHOULDER, ARM, AND HAND.

No.	Scientific Name.	Common Name or Position.
1.	Scăp'u lå	Shoulder-blade.
1.	Clăv'i cl̨e	Collar-bone.
1.	Hū'me rŭs	Upper arm.
1.	Rā'di ŭs }	Fore-arm.
1.	Ŭl'nå }	
8.	Căr'pus	Wrist.
5.	Mĕt a căr'pus	Hand.
14.	Pha lăn'ǵeṣ	Thumb and fingers.

THE TRUNK.

No.	Scientific Name.	Common Name or Position.
24.—	Vĕr′te bræ	Backbone.
24.—	Ribs	Side walls of the chest.
1.—	Stĕr′num	Breast-bone.
2.—	In nŏm i nā′tá	Hip bones.

THE LEG AND FOOT.

No.	Scientific Name.	Common Name or Position.
1.—	Fĕ′mur	Thigh.
1.—	Pa tĕl′lá	Knee-pan.
1.—	Tĭb′i á	Lower leg.
1.—	Fĭb′ū lá	
7.—	Tär′sus	Ankle.
5.—	Mĕt a tär′sus	Foot.
14.—	Pha lăn′ġĕṣ	Toes.

GENERAL DEFINITIONS.

A năt′o mў tells how the body is built and the location of its parts.

Phўs i ŏl′o gў tells the uses of each part of the body.

Hў′ġi ēne tells the conditions of health, and how to preserve it.

POSITIONS OF THE BODY.

The bones of children are easily bent out of shape by wrong positions in sitting and standing. Their feet should be supported when sitting, lest the bones of the lower limbs become bent.

The head and shoulders should be thrown back and the body held erect in walking, standing, or sitting, or the spine will become crooked.

The cushions of gristle between the vertebræ permit free and graceful motions of the body. If we stand erect, with the chin quite close to the neck, the head, without being bent forward, is perfectly balanced over our feet.

But if one has the habit of stooping forward, these cushions are so tightly pressed on the front that they lose their elasticity; then one can hardly keep erect, and we say he is "round-shouldered." Bad as this looks, it is the cause of worse trouble, as will be seen when we study the lungs.

If the body leans to one side, when one

is standing, the hip bones will soon grow out of shape. Unless careful about this, you will make your body one-sided by your position at the blackboard, or when standing to recite.

In walking, the foot expands in length and breadth. This should be remembered in buying shoes.

The heels of shoes ought to be low and broad, and placed well back; high heels crowd the foot forward and throw the whole body out of position. The shoe should be broad across the ball of the foot and the toes.

Tight shoes and high heels make the toes over-ride each other, spoil the natural beauty of the foot and the graceful carriage of the person, and are likely to cause bunions, corns, and ingrowing toe nails.

The laws of health are of much more importance than those of fashion. Children's shoes must be changed frequently for larger ones, on account of their rapidly-growing feet; if this is not done, serious injury will be the result.

TOBACCO AND THE BONES.

In whatever way tobacco may affect grown people, it is very certain that its use in childhood stunts the bones and dwarfs all the growth of the child. No boy who wants to become a full-grown, well-shaped man, can afford to smoke or chew tobacco.

Fig. 11.

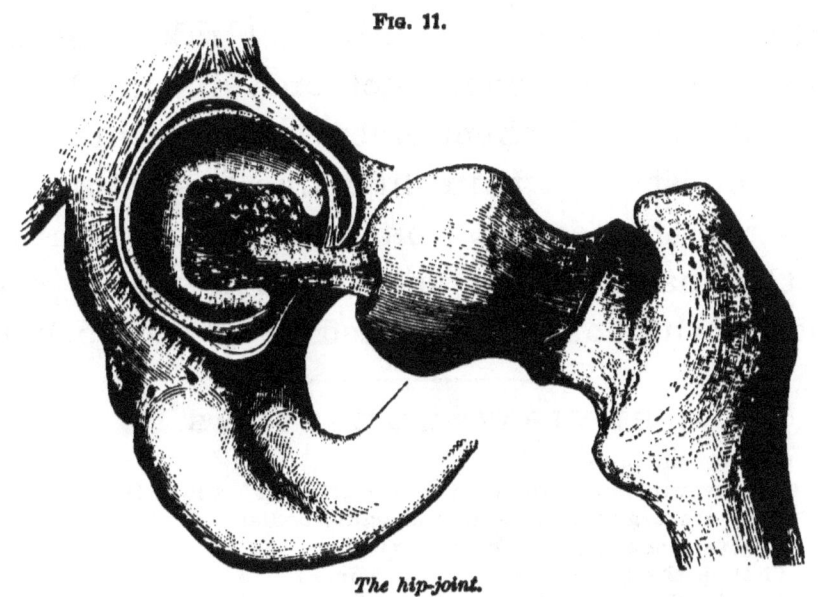

The hip-joint.

JOINTS.

A joint is the place of union of two or more bones.

At the shoulder and hip are "ball-and-socket" joints, which permit very easy movements of the arm and leg. In the fingers, wrist, and knee, are "hinge-joints," so named because the bones move backward and forward like a door upon its hinges. The bones of the head have rough edges which fit into each other, making immovable joints.

An engine must be often oiled, or it will not run properly. It can not take care of itself. But the bones not only mend themselves, but oil themselves. The joints are kept moist by a thin fluid like the white of an egg; this comes from the smooth lining of the inside of the joint; and it makes the ends of the bones move readily on each other.

REVIEW QUESTIONS.

1. What is an organ?
2. Give examples of organs in plant life—in animal life.
3. What are organic bodies?—inorganic bodies?
4. What are the uses of the bones?
5. What is the composition of the bones?
6. Why do the bones of a child not break as easily as those of an old person?
7. What mineral food is needed for the bones?
8. How is a broken bone mended?
9. How may the bones of the lower limbs be bent?
10. Define Anatomy; Physiology; Hygiene.
11. Describe the position in which one ought to stand.
12. How does tobacco affect the bones of a child?
13. What is a joint? Describe two kinds.

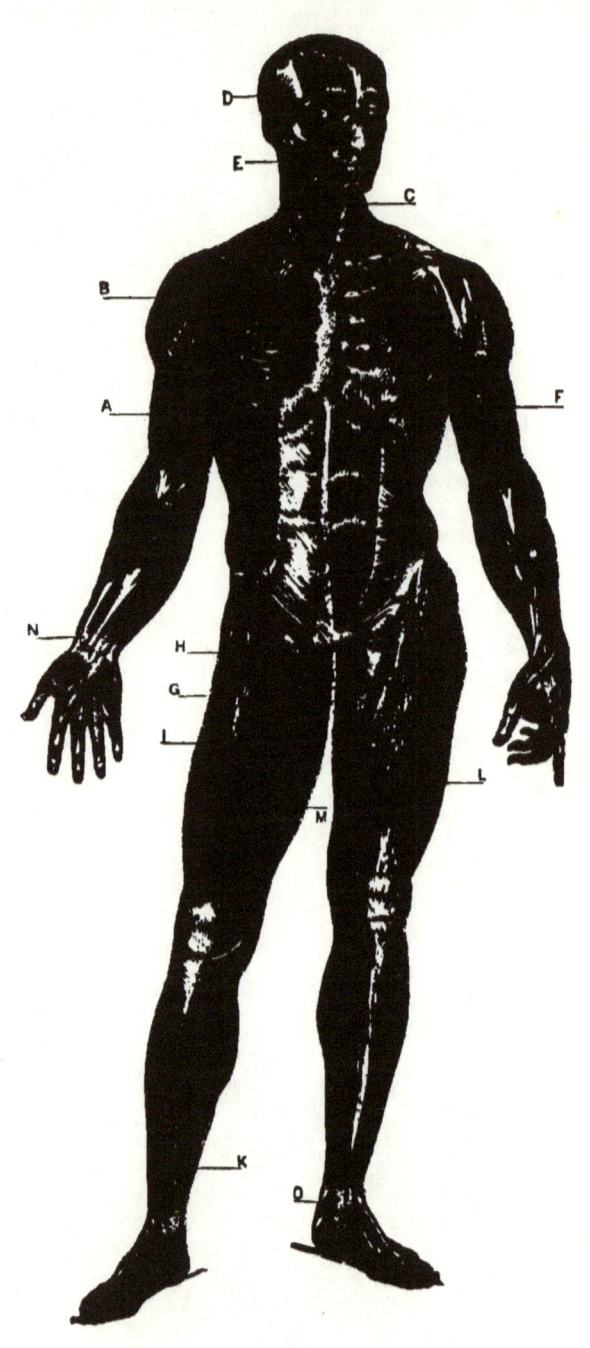

CHAPTER VII.

MUSCLES.

Fig. 12.

Tendons of the hand.

THE muscles are the flesh of the body. They consist of bundles of threads or fibers; between the fibers are blood-vessels and nerves.

The muscles are fastened to the bones by strong, tough cords, called tendons or sinews; these are easily seen, by pulling off the meat from the leg of a fowl. The "lean meat" which we eat is the flesh or muscles of the animal.

Cut, carefully, some boiled corned beef, and you can divide it into the little threads of which it is made. When people have only small, thin muscles attached to their bones, they are weak and can not do much work.

In some parts of the body, fat lies over the muscles, and is, to some extent, mingled with them. A kind of inner skin, called "connective-tissue," covers the flesh, bones, gristle, and other organs.

EXPANSION AND CONTRACTION.

When a boy raises his fore-arm, saying, "Feel my muscle," each fiber of the muscle on the front of his upper arm has shortened and thickened. This pulls up his fore-arm.

When he stretches his arm, the fibers lengthen and return to their natural shape, and a muscle on the back of the upper arm shortens and thickens in a similar way.

USES OF THE MUSCLES.

It is by means of the muscles that we keep erect, walk, run, leap, or move in any way. The motion of the many muscles of the face gives it variety of expression, showing the feelings of the mind.

Within the skeleton, in the cavities of the

trunk, there are muscles at work, without which we could not live; for instance, the heart, that sends the blood all over the body, is a strong muscle; the outer coat of the stomach has a lining of muscular fibers.

VOLUNTARY AND INVOLUNTARY MUSCLES.

Some of the muscles, as those of the arm or face, we can move when we choose, or will to do so; others, as the heart and diaphragm, keep at work without any thought of ours; they will not stop by our wishing them to.

The first are called voluntary muscles; the second, involuntary muscles.

HYGIENE OF THE MUSCLES.

Good food, pure air, and proper exercise, are necessary for muscular health. Long disuse of a muscle wastes it away. Exercise causes new fibers to form and old fibers to increase in size.

But too much, or too violent exercise is dangerous, and it is wrong to work so hard as to be always tired. Variety of exercise rests the muscles.

One who has been working with hands, or brain, all day, will be rested by a brisk out-door walk. When one has been using his lower limbs for some time, they are tired; if he then sits down, and uses his arms, or hands, and thus rests the muscles of his legs, or uses his brain in thinking or reading, he will feel refreshed.

Brisk exercise should not be taken just before, nor after a full meal. Exercise out-doors is better than exercise in-doors, and should be taken daily by all who would have good health.

KINDS OF EXERCISE.

Playing ball, rolling hoop, throwing bean-bags, coasting, skating, and swimming, are capital forms of exercise, if not carried too far.

Jumping the rope is not good exercise, for it jars the body too much, while there is great danger of catching the feet in the rope and so getting a hard fall, and, perhaps, a broken limb.

Sawing wood, and keeping the wood-box

and coal-hod filled, running home-errands with happy faces and light hearts, are healthful ways of exercise.

Cheerfulness is a great help to exercise. Whistling or singing is a good sign in a working boy or girl.

ALCOHOL AND THE MUSCLES.

Press your finger on lean beef before it is cooked, and notice how the part touched springs back when you take your finger away.

Do the same with fat meat, and you will find that a deeper dent stays there. If the flesh in your body, like the fat, could not contract, you would not be able to move.

Beer, gin, wine, cider, and all alcoholic drinks, tend more or less to change the muscles themselves to fat.

The muscles can not move and work properly, when thus changed; not only does this fat prevent their healthy action, but it is made from waste matter that should be sent out of the body.

Beer is especially bad in this respect. Beer-drinkers think they are growing strong because they grow fleshy. But they are only loading their muscles with this useless fat, which hinders instead of helping them. Beer-drinkers often die from a certain kind of heart disease, called "fatty heart."

The poor heart is not only clogged, but also weakened by this increase of fat, and the more beer one drinks, the greater the increase of fat. The heart bears this abuse as long as it can, and then it stops—the drinker is dead.

LIFE AND DEATH.

Let us try to see with "the mind's eye," the bones, the gristle, the muscles, the tendons and connective-tissue, the cavities of the head, chest, and abdomen with their organs; remember, as we look, that these are all bound together in one life.

The most wonderful thing in the living body is the mind or soul. We think at once, when we see a dead body: "How still and cold it is!" Bodily warmth and motion show life; but what life is, we have no means of knowing.

Our present study will teach us how to preserve it, and how to keep our bodies strong and healthy.

So important a subject should receive the careful attention of every one, and the rules that are of benefit to health ought to be followed.

REVIEW QUESTIONS.

1. What are muscles? Describe their structure.
2. How are muscles fastened to the bones?
3. Where is the fat of the body?
4. What is connective-tissue?
5. How do the muscles act in moving the limbs?
6. What is the special work of the muscles on the outside of the skeleton?
7. Give examples of those muscles within the skeleton.
8. Name the two classes of muscles, and define each kind.
9. What things are needed for the production of healthy muscular-tissue?
10. What are the dangers connected with exercise?
11. Is overwork wise or right?
12. How may one rest and yet keep at work?
13. When is brisk exercise unhealthful?
14. What is said of outdoor exercise?
15. Name some healthful kinds of exercise.
16. How does cheerfulness help the muscles?
17. State one difference between flesh and fat.
18. How is the action of the poison, alcohol, likely to affect muscular-tissue?
19. Does an increase of flesh always mean an increase of health? Why?

20. What is said of beer as a drink?
21. How may a "fatty heart" be caused?
22. State difference between living and dead bodies.
23. What reasons can you give for studying physiology?

CHAPTER VI.

1. What are the solid parts of the body called?
2. How many bones are there in the human skeleton?
3. Mention some of the long bones;—some short ones.
4. By what process may an egg be put into a small-necked bottle?
5. Describe the changes in the composition of the bones from infancy to old age.
6. What are the names of the bones of the arm?—of the trunk?
7. Why should the shoes of children be changed frequently?
8. What are some of the results from wearing tight shoes?

CHAPTER VIII.

FOOD.

FOOD is any substance which can be taken into the body and used for its health, life, and growth. We must have daily food to repair the daily waste of our bodies, to keep them warm, and, in childhood and youth, to make them grow.

SOURCES OF FOOD.

The earth and the air contain the materials on which our lives depend. But most of these materials must be changed in form, before they are fit for us to eat.

We hold in the hand a grain of wheat. It has no sign of life; no leaves show that it can drink in moisture and sunlight. Its outer husk is hard and dry. It seems no more alive than the grains of sand on which we are standing.

Put it into well-prepared ground. By the help of the sun, air, and moisture, it sends out rootlets into the dark earth, green shoots break through the soil, and the stem lengthens. By-and-by, a graceful plume loaded with the grain that is to make our bread, trembles in the breeze.

Down in the meadow is a beautiful carpet of green grass. It is a good place for play, but you could not eat the grass; you would starve to death if you had nothing else.

But that grass is growing, in order to make food for you. Cattle are feeding on it; it goes into their bodies, and out of it, are made the milk you drink so freely, and the flesh which may come to your table as roast beef or beefsteak.

We eat, unchanged, a few inorganic substances, or substances which have never had life, such as water and salt; but most of our food is organic—has been living,—it has been prepared by plants from the earth and air, or by animals who, by their own eating and living, have changed vegetable into animal matter.

KINDS OF FOOD.

Our food is divided into three great classes—

1st.—Mineral food.

2d.—Food like the whites of eggs, or lean meat, which is needed for the growth or repair of the various parts of the body; it is sometimes called tissue-making food.

3d.—Fats or oils, starch and sugar.

MINERAL FOOD.

This includes all inorganic substances that we eat unchanged, together with some that we get in other kinds of food. The most important of these are water and salt.

If a man weigh 160 pounds, about 140 pounds of this weight is nothing but water— "quite enough, if rightly arranged, to drown him."

Much of this is in the blood, some in the muscles, some in the tears, and the rest in other parts of the body, as you will learn by further study. It dissolves other food, so that the body can use it, and helps to regulate the heat of the system.

We must have water to drink, and it should be pure and good. Death from thirst is quicker and more painful than death from lack of food.

We do not drink all the water which the body requires; for we get a large part of the amount needed in the food itself, as in fruits and vegetables, the juices of meat, milk, and the water used in cooking these.

PURITY OF WATER.

Water that runs through lead pipes, is very likely to dissolve some of the lead, if it stands in the pipes for any length of time.

Lead is a very sure poison. Care must be taken to draw off all the water that has so stood, so as to avoid danger. You will learn more about poisoned water in the chapter on respiration.

SALT.

Watch the sheep when the farmer "salts" them, and see how eager they are for the treat. Salt is necessary to man, as well as to the lower animals; but it exists naturally in most food-materials. A moderate amount of it, as seasoning, makes our food more agreeable and healthful.

LIME, PHOSPHORUS, AND IRON.

The bones need lime, the brain requires phosphorus, and the blood must have iron, in order to be perfectly healthy.

But we can not eat clear lime, phosphorus, or iron. We must get them by eating vegetables which have taken these minerals from the ground and made them into material fit for our use, or by eating the flesh of animals which have fed upon such vegetables.

TISSUE-MAKING FOODS.

Among the most important of these are milk and the grains; they are found, too, in eggs and the different kinds of meat.

Wheat contains more of these foods than other common grains, and bread made from this grain is most nourishing and best.

FATS OR OILS, STARCH AND SUGAR.

These are used, in part, for the growth and repair of the body; but they are of especial use in keeping the body warm.

THE FATS OR OILS.

These are found in both animal and vegetable food; for example, beef and mutton suets, the cream of milk, the yolks of eggs, Indian corn, olive and palm oils.

People who live in cold climates need and crave much of this kind of food.

A story is told of some English sailors who prepared a "Christmas tree," as a treat for a company of Esquimau children. As no suitable tree could be had, they made an imitation one, by tying together walrus bones, shaping the whole to look as much as possible like a tree.

Instead of candy, they made some balls of whale blubber and hung them on the "tree." The children were delighted and ate the balls of fat as eagerly as you eat your Christmas candies.

Some food of this kind is necessary; and,

if one does not like it, he should learn to eat enough of it for health.

Those who do not eat fats of any kind, are usually thin and unhealthy and likely to have some serious disease, as scrofula or consumption, even while young. Butter may be used instead of fat meat if preferred. On the other hand, too much fat must not be eaten; a naturally fleshy person requires less than the average amount.

STARCH.

Starch forms a large part of most grains, seeds, roots, and unripe fruits. As you know, it must be cooked, or, in fruits and nuts, ripened, before it is fit for food.

Corn-starch and potato-starch are in common use by the cook and laundress. Rice, the chief food of the people of India, China, and Japan, is three-quarters starch. Unripe fruits, as green apples, contain so much starch that they are very likely to make you sick if you eat them uncooked.

All starchy foods, as those from the grains, require long and thorough cooking to make them more easily digested and more nourishing.

Gum resembles starch, but is less nutritious. Some kinds, as gum arabic, are used for food in Eastern countries.

SUGAR.

Sugar is an important article of food. But a person would, in time, starve to death if fed alone on either sugar or starch.

Too much sugar is often eaten in the form of candy, and does much harm when eaten between meals. Injurious substances are often put into candy, to give it color or increase its weight. The results of eating much candy are a "sour stomach," "bad breath," and other serious troubles.

The coloring matter in candies is often really poisonous, and even the white candy, usually considered the purest, is sometimes largely made of "terra alba" (tĕr′rà ăl′bà), a kind of white earth.

Put a piece of candy into a tumbler with a little water; if it is not pure, when the sugar has dissolved, the terra alba will sink to the bottom of the tumbler in the form of a white powder.

Thus you can easily prove whether you are eating sugar, or a substance that is worse than useless, because it clogs the body.

MILK.

Milk is the only food provided by nature for young children. Since the child lives and grows upon it, we should expect milk to contain, as it does, the different classes of food.

The cream is fat, or heat-forming substance; the curd, which can be pressed into cheese, belongs to the tissue-making foods; there is enough sugar to give it a sweet taste, and it contains lime and other minerals needed to sustain healthy life, besides water, of which it has 88 parts in 100.

WHAT TO EAT.

Most people, in temperate climates, eat both animal and vegetable food. You will usually find the three great classes of food on the dinner-tables of your homes.

Water and salt are mineral foods; potatoes and meat, heat and tissue-making foods. Most persons crave the fat of butter with the starch of bread.

Pepper, mustard, and vinegar, are not needed in building up the body and should be very sparingly used, if at all. Probably a perfectly natural and healthy appetite would not crave them.

If the system needs acids, lemons and limes, which are more healthful than vinegar, may be eaten. Fresh, ripe fruit which generally contains some acid, is wholesome when too much is not taken.

TEA AND COFFEE.

The value of these to adults is doubted by many wise physicians. Certainly they are not necessary or safe drinks for children.

COOKING.

Health is, in great measure, dependent upon the way in which our food is cooked. Meat should be boiled, roasted, or broiled. Neither meat nor any other food should be fried: heated fat hardens whatever is cooked in it, making it difficult of digestion.

To eat or drink what we know is unhealthful, because it tastes good, is not only foolish but wicked.

A cook who well understands the laws of health, will not feed the family on hot bread, because it makes a pasty mass in the stomach which can not easily be digested.

Instead of rich pastry, and cake heavy with fruit and spices, which overload the stomach and unfit it for proper work, juicy meat, mealy potatoes, ripe fruit, and light, sweet bread, will be prepared. The latter, when it is made from the whole wheat, ground, forms, with the addition of butter, and some water to satisfy thirst, a perfect food.

In "bolting," the phosphorus and much of the flesh-making part of the grain is lost. Fine wheat flour is not so nourishing for the brain and muscles, as that flour which contains some of the outer portion of the kernel.

FRUITS.

Ripe fruits, such as apples, oranges, bananas, and berries, make the most healthful "dessert." The skins, cores, and seeds should not be swallowed, as they are useless and may cause trouble if eaten.

REVIEW QUESTIONS.

1. What is food?
2. State three ways in which it is used by our bodies.
3. What names are given to the three classes of food?
4. Name the three principal mineral foods.
5. Do we need to drink all the water the body requires?
6. What care should be taken in the use of lead water-pipes?
7. How do we get salt, lime, and other mineral substances for our bodies?
8. Name the principal tissue-making foods;—heat-making foods.
9. Where are fats or oils found?
10. Is it necessary to eat fat of some kind?
11. How is starch made fit for food?
12. Why is green food likely to make one sick?
13. What are the results of eating too much sugar?
14. Show that all three classes of food are contained in milk.
15. Are pepper, mustard, and vinegar, essential to health?
16. Why should a cook understand the laws of health?
17. Why is whole wheat flour better food than finely bolted flour?

CHAPTER IX.

ARE NARCOTICS FOODS?

IS ALCOHOL FOOD?

A PERFECT food, as we have seen in the case of milk, contains water, tissue-making, and heat-making materials.

Alcohol is not a food, for it can not build up any part of the body. It contains no mineral substance, and will not make healthy fat.

Materials in the blood which should make muscles, bone, etc., as well as those which should be sent out of the body, are sometimes changed into useless fat by the action of alcohol. The heat of the body is lessened by alcohol, instead of being increased.

IS BEER FOOD?

Beer is made from water, malt, hops, and yeast. Water can be obtained better and cheaper elsewhere. The starch of the grain, you remember, was changed into sugar by malting, and the sugar turned into alcohol by fermentation, thus losing its food nature.

The gummy substance left after the starch turned to sugar and then to alcohol, and the hops, may contain a slight amount of material that the body can use. But the amount of food in beer is so very small, as scarcely to be worth taking into account in speaking of its effects.

"As much flour as can lie on the point of a table-knife is more nutritious than eight quarts of the best Bavarian beer." (Liebig.)

A man gets one glass of pure alcohol in every twenty glasses of lager-beer that he drinks; in the stronger beer, one glass of alcohol to thirteen of beer.

There is no truth, you see, in the claim that beer makes one stronger. There is no food in it worth mentioning, and its alcohol does a vast amount of harm.

IS WINE FOOD?

A few raisins contain more nourishment than much wine. Sugar in fruit-juice becomes alcohol by fermentation; it is the alcohol, which is not food, that the wine-drinker wants. Often more alcohol is added to the wine made from pure fruit-juice, to satisfy the craving for a stronger drink.

The more sugar there is in a liquid undergoing vinous fermentation, the more alcohol will it produce. Sweet apples and sweet grapes make strong cider and strong wine. Currant, gooseberry, elderberry, and other home-made wines, sometimes contain even more alcohol than the wines of commerce, because sugar is added to the fermenting juices.

Cider and these home-made wines contain the merest trifle of food-material, and are no more "innocent drinks" than port or champagne (shăm păn'). The poison, alcohol, is there, ready to do its deadly work.

People not only become intoxicated by drinking these wines; but, by their use, a craving is often created for stronger drinks—that is, those which contain more alcohol.

By drinking a larger quantity of the

weaker liquors, the user gets the alcohol his increasing appetite demands. This is especially true of beer-drinkers.

IS CIDER FOOD?

Cider is a fermented drink made from the juice of apples. In the open air, at summer heat, apple-juice begins to ferment in about six hours after it is drawn off from the pulp, and sometimes sooner.

A little juice often remains in the cider-mill after a previous grinding. If this ferments and is allowed to remain, it will act as yeast, hastening fermentation in the juice of the next lot of apples ground.

When little bubbles begin to pass through the liquid and break at the top, as the froth gathers, we may know that the sugar is turning to alcohol. The bubbles are the escaping carbonic acid gas.

If the apples are fairly sweet, alcohol will form until in ten cups of hard cider, there will be one cup of pure alcohol. Thus the barrel of cider that may possibly have been sweet, when it was put into the cellar, gains in alcohol every day, until it begins to turn to vinegar.

Cider is mainly water and alcohol. As the latter is a poison, the old custom of considering the barrel of cider as important a part of the family food as the barrel of flour, had no truth for its foundation.

There is great danger that the cider-drinker will learn to crave a stronger drink, because alcohol makes those who drink it thirsty for more. Many of those who die as drunkards in this country, began their course at the cider barrel.

If the people who drink cider for its acid taste and effect, would take lemon or lime-juice instead, they would get the acid without the poison of alcohol.

STIMULANTS.

"Alcohol* never acts as any thing but

---

*Alcohol has been falsely called a stimulant, because it sometimes makes the person who takes it feel stronger, and seem more quick-witted and talkative, for a short time. But a reaction follows, just in proportion to the amount of excitement there has been, and the person is more or less weak and depressed.

Whipping a horse causes him to move faster for a while; yet it gives no fresh strength to the animal, but rather uses up that a paralyzer."—*Dr. James Edmunds.* "Alcohol has clearly no right to be called a stimulant."—*Dr. J. J. Ridge.*

People have called alcohol a stimulant, because they were ignorant of its real nature. It gives the body no added strength; its only effect on pain and fatigue is the deadening of the nerves, so that one does not realize the disordered, exhausted condition of his body.*

The apparent increase of energy which alcohol gives, is due to the partial paralysis of a certain class of nerves in the body which act as its "brakes." Alcohol, there-

---

which he already possessed, so that he overworks and is more tired as the result. Spurring to increased action without giving any food which the body can use to balance the extra "wear and tear," is not the action of a true stimulant, and the term is wrongly used when thus applied.

*Suppose, for instance, you measure your muscular strength with a health-lift, and then take some of the drink which you think will give you power. When you feel strong, measure your strength again. The drink has fooled you, that is all. You felt that you were stronger than natural; you find that the narcotic has been true to its paralyzing nature and that you are weaker.

Then, after a time, when the drug has spent itself and you feel weak and prostrated, measure your strength once more. Fooled again; the stuff has fooled you twice. When you felt yourself strong, you were weak; and now, when you feel yourself weak, you find yourself really stronger, for your natural strength is returning.—*Adapted from Dr. A. F. Kinne.*

fore, is not a stimulant in the proper sense of that word.

ALCOHOL AND WORK.

A vessel coming from Australia sprung a leak soon after starting, and the men had to work at the pumps all the way home.

At first, regular rations of liquor were given; but the sailors soon began to grow weak and tired. Then the captain stopped the use of liquor, giving an extra supply of food, instead. At once, the men began to sleep well and to waken strong and rested.

In spite of the hard work at the pumps, the crew were in good health when they reached England. The liquor deadened—narcotized—the nerves which control muscular action, and the men lost strength thereby; the food furnished building material for their bodies and so increased their working power.

"The following statement was made by Sir William Fairbairn, an eminent engineer of Manchester, England, when at the head of a firm employing between one and two thousand workmen:

"'I strictly prohibit on my works the use of beer or fermented liquors of any sort, or of tobacco. I enforce the prohibition of alcoholic drinks so strongly, that if I found any man transgressing the rule in that respect, I would instantly discharge him.'

"The reasons for these measures are thus stated:

"'In those foundries in which there is drinking throughout the works all day long, it is observed of the men employed as workmen, that they do not work so well; their perceptions are clouded, and they are stupefied and heavy.

"'I have provided water for the use of the men in every department of the works. In summer-time, the men engaged in the strongest work, such as strikers to the heavy forges, drink water very copiously.

"'I am convinced that workmen who drink water are really more active and do more work, and are more healthy than those who drink alcoholic liquors.'

"This is the testimony of all accurate observers."—*Dr. A. B. Palmer.*

Observation of the effects of alcohol shows us—

1st.—That the healthy action of the muscles is hindered by the useless fat formed through the influence of alcohol.

2d.—That the nerves are deadened.

3d.—That strength is lost rather than gained by the drinking of alcoholic liquors.

REVIEW QUESTIONS.

1. What does a perfect food contain?
2. Can alcohol do the work of any of the three classes of food?
3. How does it act to make one fleshy?
4. How does it affect the heat of the body?
5. Compare the food-materials in beer and bread.
6. How much alcohol is there in lager-beer?
7. How much in the stronger beers?
8. What harm may this do to the drinker?
9. How is wine made?
10. Do "home-made wines" contain alcohol?
11. Are they nourishing?
12. How is cider made?
13. How much alcohol is there in hard cider?
14. Is cider food?
15. Why do cider-drinkers often become drunkards?
16. What acids are more healthful than cider?
17. Why has alcohol been called a stimulant?
18. What is its effect on pain and fatigue?
19. How does it seem to increase one's energy?

20. Why is alcohol not a true stimulant?
21. Does alcohol give strength for work? Illustrate.
22. Give Sir Wm. Fairbairn's statements in regard to the use of alcohol and tobacco by the men in his workshops.

CHAPTER VII.

1. What kind of meat are the muscles called?
2. Show how the size of the muscles affects one's strength.
3. What is the effect of disuse upon a muscle?
4. How does variety of exercise affect the muscles?
5. What are the best times for exercise?
6. How does an increase of fat sometimes affect the heart?

CHAPTER X.

DIGESTION.

HUNGER and thirst are cries of the whole body for food and water, though only the throat seems to call for the water and the stomach for the food.

Digestion is the preparation of the food which has been taken into the stomach, for the use of the body.

Many wonderful changes must take place, before the beef, potatoes, bread, water, and other food which we eat, can become solid bone and liquid blood, strong muscle, working hand, and thinking brain.

WASTE AND REPAIR.

Tearing down and building up—making and unmaking—these two processes are always going on within us.

If you stand by a city market, early on a summer morning, you may see carts bringing green peas, fresh meat, milk, and other food, from the country farms. Other carts, at the same time, are carrying off barrels of ashes, bones, scraps of food, and other waste matter. They will dump this stuff far enough from the city to prevent any harm to the people from its decay.

Work very much like this goes on in your body. There are certain vessels whose special duty it is to carry the prepared food to the different organs, and others that are the scavengers of the human system.

If you should stop eating, you would starve to death in a short time; if you should keep the waste matter in your body, instead of letting it pass out through the skin, lungs, kidneys, and other organs, you would die even more quickly.

ORGANS OF DIGESTION.

The principal organs of digestion are the mouth, gullet or esophagus (ê sŏph'a ğŭs), stomach (stŏm'ach), and intestines (ĭn tĕs'tĭnĕs). Taken together, these are often called the food-canal.

This canal, in a full-grown person, is about thirty feet long. Here and there, beside it, are little fleshy bags called glands; these glands have the curious power of separating certain juices from the blood; this is called secretion (sē-crē′tion).

It is these juices which digest the food. A tongue much coated shows that other portions of the food-canal, as well as the part which we can see, are out of order.

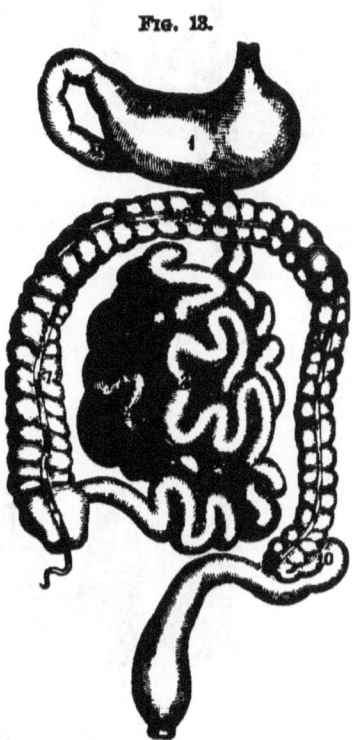

The stomach and intestines. 1, *stomach*; 3, *small intestine*; 7, 8, 9, 10, *large intestine.*

THE TEETH.

The mouth, with its fixed roof and movable floor, takes in the food; the tongue, cheeks, and jaws, move it backward and forward, up and down; the teeth cut and grind it. This should be well done, because the digestive juices can not mix quickly or properly with lumps of food. A child has twenty teeth; these last for a few years, and are then pushed out by the growth of others behind them. This second set numbers thirty-two in all—sixteen in each jaw.

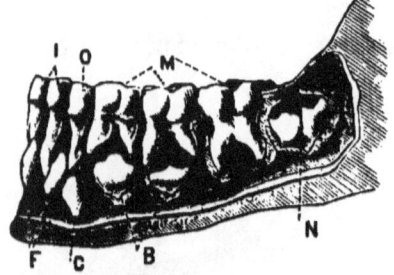

Fig. 14.

The teeth at the age of six and one-half years. I, the cutting teeth; M, the grinding teeth; F, C, B, N, the new or second set of teeth.

Those in front are sharp and of use in biting. The back teeth are broad and are

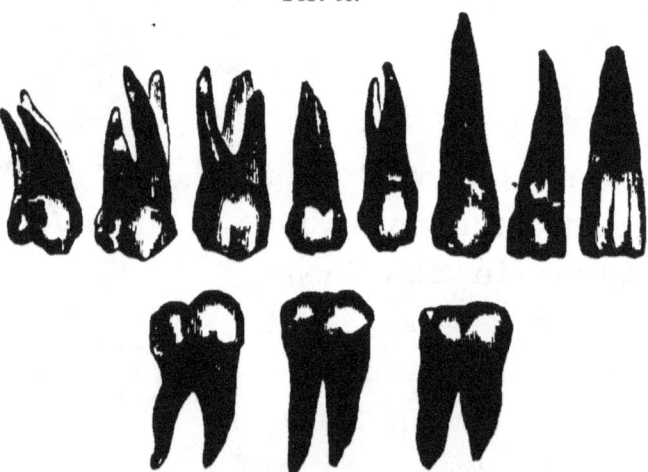

Fig. 15.

Different kinds of teeth.

much used in chewing; they are fastened

CARE OF THE TEETH.

into the jaws by two or three roots, while the front teeth have each but one root.

The bone of a tooth is covered with a hard, smooth coating, called enamel (en ăm'el), which protects it. If this enamel is broken in any way, the teeth are likely to decay and to cause a great deal of trouble and pain.

CARE OF THE TEETH.

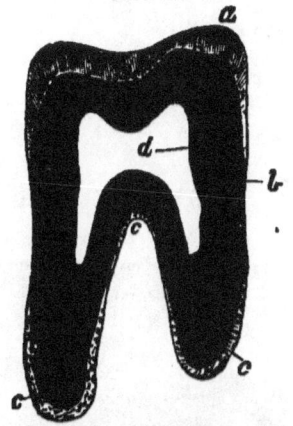

Fig. 16.

Vertical section of a molar tooth, moderately magnified. a, enamel of the crown, the lines of which indicate the arrangement of its columns; b, dentine; c, cement; d, pulp cavity.

If you wish to have good teeth and to escape the pains of toothache — brush your teeth after each meal, and pick them, if necessary to remove particles of food, with a quill or wooden tooth-pick — never with a pin, lest you break the enamel. For the same reason, never use the teeth to crack nuts or bite thread. "Better to take pains than to have pains take you."

It is very warm in the mouth — nearly 100° by the thermometer, as warm as the air on a hot July day. At that temperature, a piece of meat would spoil in twenty-four hours.

DIGESTION.

If we eat meat, therefore, the little pieces which get between our teeth, if not removed, will soon begin to decay in this warm place, and so injure the teeth and gums.

THE SALIVARY GLANDS.

Three pairs of glands—one near and below the ears,* one pair under the tongue, and one pair under the lower jaw—aided by other very small glands that line the inside of the cheeks, pour out a juice called saliva (sa li′vá), which not only moistens the food, but transforms some of its starch into sugar.

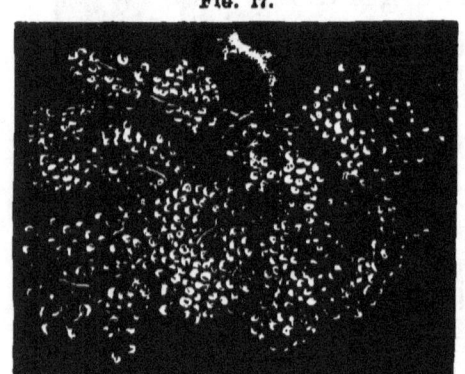

Fig. 17.

The parotid—one of the salivary glands.

This is the first of the great changes which take place in food during the process of digestion. You will see how important

---

* It is the glands under the ears—the parotid (pa rŏt′ id) glands—that swell and are so painful when one has the mumps.

THE SALIVARY GLANDS.

it is that the work of the saliva should be thoroughly done, when you remember that unchanged starch does not nourish the body; if not changed in the mouth, it must be changed, but with more difficulty, elsewhere in the food-canal.

"Washing down the food," even with pure water, will not take the place of slow eating, by which the starch is thoroughly mixed with the saliva and thus changed to sugar. Water simply moistens the food so that it can be more easily swallowed.

If the work of the mouth is but partly done, as by rapid eating, the other organs have more than their share to do; they may soon break down, and their owner suffers from dyspepsia (dўs pĕp' sĭ ȧ), or some similar disease.

You may prove that starch is changed to sugar in the mouth, by chewing slowly a piece of dry cracker and noticing how sweet it tastes.

To say that "the mouth waters," is often exactly true. When we think of some favorite food, especially if hungry, the glands may send an extra amount of saliva into the mouth, as if the food was there ready for its action.

TOBACCO AND THE MOUTH.

Sores on the lips, and even cancers, sometimes result from the use of tobacco; the breath, foul and repulsive, shows the condition of the stomach, the tissues, and the blood; the gums of smokers and chewers often become spongy, and their teeth are soiled and dark, instead of being white and pure.

The effect of the poison is to make the mouth dry, thus causing an extra amount of saliva to be poured out from the glands. But the constant spitting of the tobacco juice, robs one of the saliva needed for digestion, and thus brings on dyspepsia.

Besides doing this harm to the user, the habit of spitting is a very impolite one. It makes floors and sidewalks unfit for cleanly people to walk on, and endangers the clothing of all who are near.

A man who should spit directly at another would be thought very insulting. Is he respecting the rights of others, though he may not intend to insult them, when he sends the foul juice a little to one side—or where they must tread at the next step?

In many cases, tobacco acts as the usher at the door of the saloon, because the dryness of the mouth which it produces, makes the user thirsty. But it is not a natural thirst,—it can not be satisfied by water; for tobacco so affects the nerves, as often to make one crave another narcotic.

Those in charge of inebriate asylums say that nearly all their patients have been users of tobacco as well as of alcohol.

THE ESOPHAGUS.

When divided by the teeth and softened and changed by the saliva, the food is ready to be swallowed, or sent into the esophagus, the passage-way to the stomach.

Look at the throat of a horse when he is drinking, and you will see the motion of the ring-shaped muscles of this tube.

Food and drink do not simply slide down the esophagus; a horse often bends his head when he drinks, so that his mouth is really lower than his stomach.

The muscles contract, one after the other, and push the food gently onward. For this reason, a juggler is able to perform the common trick of drinking a glass of water, while standing on his head.

THE STOMACH.

The stomach is a strong muscular bag in the left side of the abdomen (ab dŏ′ men). Its inner lining has many glands which separate from the blood a juice, called gastric juice. In this is a substance named pepsin (pĕp′ sĭn), which digests the flesh-making parts of our food.

The next coat contains muscular fibers. These stretch and shrink in such a way, that the food is gently moved from one end of the stomach to the other, and so forced to mix with the gastric juice.

Some parts of the food are ready for use when they enter the stomach. These are at once taken up by tiny blood-vessels, carried to the liver, and then to the heart. The process by which food-materials enter the blood, is called absorption (ab sôrp′shŭn).

When the work of the stomach is ended, the food which is left is a grayish fluid, called chyme (kīm.) It consists largely of the tissue-making substances, and the fats that have been eaten. A part of the starch and sugar, after being prepared in the mouth, has already entered the blood.

THE INTESTINES.

This part of the food-canal is a small tube, about twenty-five feet long in an adult, coiled very closely in the abdomen. You will understand it better by looking at the intestines of a chicken, when the cook is "drawing" it in the kitchen.

Much remains to be done before the chyme is ready to enter the blood. The glands of the intestines are helped by two other glands which lie in the abdomen, one on the right side of the body—the liver, and the other toward the left—the pancreas (păn′ cre ăs).

These send into the intestines, through a

small tube, the bile and the pancreatic (păn ere ăt'ĭc) juice, which, with the intestinal juices, divide and prepare the fats.

If the mouth, or the stomach, has failed in any part of its work, these juices in the intestines do their best to complete the task. They can often do but little, however, and so we may lose part of the value of the food.

When fully digested, the milky mass is called chyle (kīl), and is ready to enter the blood. It does this by soaking through the thin walls of blood-vessels and tiny tubes called lacteals (lăc'tĕ ăls).

STEPS OF DIGESTION.

In a large factory, each man has a special task to perform; the spinners do not attend to the looms, the weavers have nothing to do in the engine-room. So in the body, each part has its own work.

The saliva, to an extent, digests the starch foods. The gastric juice digests the tissue-making foods. The bile and pancreatic juice digest the fats.

If one must eat rapidly, as at a railroad station, the meal should be mainly of meat, as that will give strength and need not be mixed with the saliva for digestion.

The heat of the stomach must be over 100°, in order to digest the food properly. Ice-water at once lowers the temperature: if taken too freely at meals, the stomach must stop working until it can get "warmed up" again. Such delays in the process of digestion are injurious.

MEALS.

Most healthy persons have three meals a day, at intervals of five or six hours. Since the stomach, like other muscles, needs rest, one should not eat between meals. The mind either helps or hinders the body: the food digests much more readily if there is pleasant, cheerful thought and talk at the table.

An old Eastern story tells of a stranger who met the Plague coming from Bagdad.

"You have been committing great havoc there," said the trader, pointing to the city.

"Not so great," replied the Plague; "I

killed only one-third of those who died; the other two-thirds killed themselves with fright."

ALCOHOL AND THE STOMACH.

As soon as alcohol enters this organ, it is hurried on into the blood-vessels; for the stomach knows it can not be digested, and is useless to the body. But the very short time it stays there, is enough to cause great harm.

It can not pass through the thin walls of the blood-vessels unless mixed with water. It needs even more water than was contained in the liquors which were drunk; so it shrinks and thickens the delicate lining of the stomach, by robbing it of its moisture. In health, this lining is slightly red, tinged with yellow.

The blood does not move properly, or as it should, in the blood-vessels of even the "moderate drinker," and those in the stomach soon become swollen. In the drunkard, the case is likely to be still worse; for sores sometimes appear on the walls of the stomach. If one stops drinking liquors which contain alcohol, these will be cured. They do not pain the drinker as they would if on the surface of the body, for reasons which you will understand when you study the nerves.

Sickness, thirst, headache, coated tongue, feverish pulse, go with these conditions of the stomach. The only possible cure is to stop drinking liquor at once and forever.

There is enough alcohol in strong spirits to harden the tissue-making foods, which must be changed to a liquid form in the stomach, before they can be absorbed.

Alcohol, of any considerable strength, separates the pepsin from the gastric juice and prevents its proper action on the food.

Dr. Munroe, of England, proved this by an interesting experiment. He put equal quantities of finely-minced beef into three bottles. Then into one, he poured water and gastric juice from the stomach of a calf; into another, alcohol with gastric juice; and into the third, pale ale and gastric juice.

The bottles were kept at the same heat as the human stomach, and the contents moved about like those of that organ.

DIGESTION.

The following table shows the results:

Finely-minced Beef.	2d Hour.	4th Hour.	6th Hour.	8th Hour.	10th Hour.
1st. Bottle. Gastric juice and water.	Beef becomes opaque.	Beef separating.	Beef much less in quantity.	Beef broken into shreds.	Beef dissolved as in soup.
2d. Bottle. Gastric juice and alcohol.	No change.	No change.	Slight coating on beef.	No change.	Beef solid on cooling. Pepsin separated from the gastric juice.
3d. Bottle. Gastric juice and ale.	No change.	Cloudy with coating on beef.	Beef partly loosened.	No change.	Beef not digested. Pepsin separated from the gastric juice.

Study this table carefully, and see how the clear alcohol and that in the ale, destroyed the power of the gastric juice, by taking out the pepsin from it. It often has a similar effect on that in the stomach, though it remains there but a short time.

SEEING DIGESTION.

By this time you wonder, perhaps, how all these things are known, when the stomach is covered up in our bodies.

Some of them the doctors have learned by studying the stomachs of dead persons. But there has been one good chance to look into a live man's stomach and see what was going on there.

In 1822, a man named Alexis St. Martin, was shot in his left side. When the wound healed, it left a hole in his stomach, partly closed by a fold of the inner lining. This could be pushed aside, so that one could look directly into the stomach.

By this means, the doctor who had charge of him, learned much about the digestion of food, and the effects of alcohol upon the stomach. Later experiments upon the stomachs of living men and of the lower animals, have taught us much more on this subject.

TOBACCO AND THE STOMACH.

As already said, the nicotine of tobacco is almost sure to cause sickness of the stomach and vomiting, in those who are just beginning to use the poison. It injures the lining of the stomach, hinders the flow of the gastric juice, and, in this manner, seriously interferes with digestion.

Dr. B. W. Richardson says: "One who smokes a pipe is very likely to have dyspepsia."

OPIUM, CHLORAL, AND THE STOMACH.

The stomach of the opium-eater, and of the user of chloral, soon has its digestive power impaired.

OTHER ORGANS OF THE ABDOMEN.

THE LIVER.

This is the largest organ in the body and one of the most important. It fills the whole of the right and upper side of the abdomen. One part of its work is to secrete the bile, or gall, used in digestion.

This juice, when not needed, is stored in a little sac, called the gall-bladder. It is of a dark yellow color, and "bitter as gall" is a common proverb.

The liver also changes, in some way not clearly understood, the chyme brought to it from the stomach, aids in the manufacture of blood, and in the preparation of worn-out materials for removal from the body.

ALCOHOL AND THE LIVER.

While we can not fully explain all its action, we know that diseases of the liver affect all the other organs.

More alcohol goes to the liver and brain than to any other parts of the body. By it, the gall may be changed from yellow to green or black, and from a thin fluid to a thick one.

The liver itself often becomes twice its natural size; in other cases, it is filled with useless fat, like the muscles. When rough and shrunken, with hard lumps or knots, it is called by the English, "hob-nailed," or "gin liver." This condition is caused only by alcohol and is incurable.

The coal-heavers of London drink a great deal of gin, whiskey, and ale. They seem strong, but they often sicken and die from a mere scratch. Their blood is so poisoned from their diseased livers that the wound festers, does not readily heal, and frequently proves fatal.

THE KIDNEYS.

These are two oval glands at the back of the abdomen, that carry a large part of the waste matter out of the body.

ALCOHOL AND THE KIDNEYS.

A serious, because usually fatal, sickness, is called "Bright's disease of the kidneys." This may be caused in many ways; but it is most often the result of alcoholic drinks, especially if combined with exposure to wet and cold.

"**Water** supplies every necessity as a fluid for the body."*

Alcohol robs the body of water and can not be used by it as a fluid.

Water dissolves other foods.

Alcohol hardens tissue-making foods, and has no power to dissolve any of the food-materials.

Water helps the digestive juices.

Alcohol separates pepsin from the gastric

---
* Dr. B. W. Richardson.

juice, coagulates it, and thus interferes with digestion.

Water carries the digested foods into the blood.

Alcohol hinders the digested foods from entering the blood.

Water is the proper liquid of the blood.

Alcohol is injurious to the blood.

Water satisfies our thirst.

Alcohol does not satisfy thirst, but creates a strong craving for itself.

Water, taken in proper quantities, is a healthful food.

Alcohol, taken in any quantity, injures the body in proportion to the amount taken.

REVIEW QUESTIONS.

1. What is digestion?
2. What two kinds of work go on in the body?
3. What would happen if you were to stop taking food?—if you should prevent the waste matter from leaving your body?
4. Why is a child's face plump, and an old man's wrinkled?
5. Name the organs of digestion.
6. What are glands, and what is their work?
7. How many teeth has a child?—an adult?
8. Describe the teeth.
9. How should the teeth be taken care of?
10. Where are the salivary glands?

11. What is the action of the saliva on the food?
12. Prove that starch may be changed to sugar in the mouth.
13. What are the effects of tobacco on the mouth?
14. What do you think of the habit of spitting?
15. What is the relation of tobacco to alcohol?
16. How do we swallow our food?
17. Describe the stomach. Name its digestive juice.
18. What is the action of the gastric juice on the food?
19. What is absorption?
20. What kinds of food enter the blood from the stomach?
21. Describe the intestines.
22. What juices mix with the partly-digested food in the intestines?
23. What is their action on the food?
24. How does the chyle enter the blood-vessels and lacteals?
25. State the steps of digestion.
26. If obliged to eat in haste, what food would you choose? Why?
27. What is the effect of drinking large quantities of ice-water?
28. How often should one eat?
29. Why should the meal-time be made a pleasant time?
30. How does alcohol often affect the walls of the stomach?
31. What is its effect on the gastric juice? Illustrate by Dr. Monroe's experiment.
32. Give the story of Alexis St. Martin.
33. What are the effects of tobacco, opium, and chloral on the stomach?

OTHER ORGANS OF THE ABDOMEN.

34. Describe the liver;—the gall.
35. What are the effects of alcohol on the liver and gall?
36. What is the "gin liver"?
37. Why are slight wounds often dangerous to drinking men?
38. What is a common effect of alcohol on the kidneys?
39. Contrast the effects of water and alcohol.

CHAPTER XI.

RESPIRATION.

INSPIRATION AND EXPIRATION.

PLACE your hands firmly against your sides, and draw long, deep breaths. Notice that the side walls of your chest are not fixed, but move out and in, as you breathe, about eighteen times a minute.

Hold your hand close before your face, and you will feel a current of air upon it, as the ribs move in. Breathe upon a mirror, and a thin film of water covers it, coming from your breath. On a cold winter day, this partly freezes, and you say you can "see your breath."

The diaphragm is a strong muscle which forms the partition between the chest and the abdomen. When the ribs move outward, this moves downward, and air enters your chest through the organs of breathing; this is called inspiration (ĭn spĭ rā′ tion).

When the ribs move back into position, and the diaphragm moves upward, the air

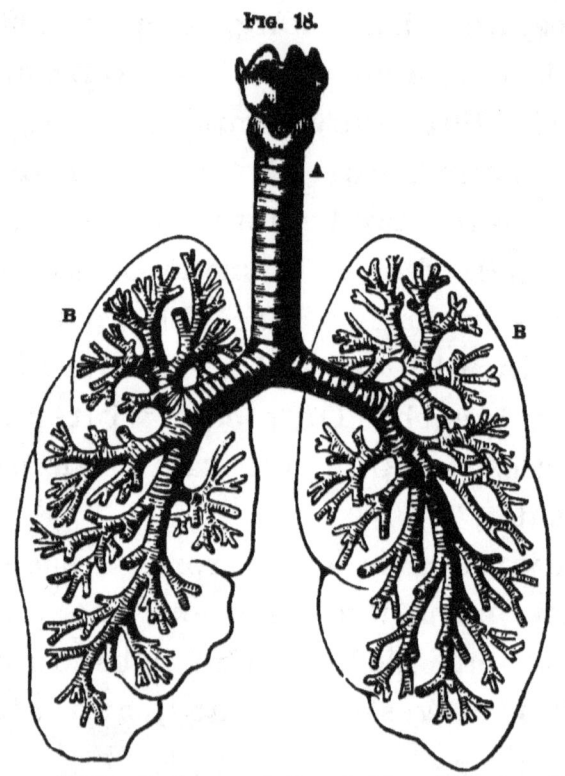

FIG. 18.

The lungs, showing the larynx. A, the windpipe; B, the bronchial tubes.

is forced out, bringing with it water and other waste material; this is called expiration (ĕx pĭ rā′ tion). Taken together, these make up breathing or respiration (rĕs pĭ rā′ tion).

ORGANS OF BREATHING.

The organs of breathing are the nose and mouth, through which air enters the body, the larynx (lăr′ ўnx), windpipe, bronchial (brŏn′-kĭ al) tubes, and lungs.

LARYNX AND WINDPIPE.

From the back of the mouth, the air passes down a straight tube at the front of the chest, called the windpipe or trachea (tra′-kē à). This is made of ring-shaped cartilages and is easily felt through the skin of the neck. Its upper end is the larynx, the organ of voice.

The larynx swells out at the front, is larger in men than in women, and is sometimes called, "Adam's apple." It is a tube-like box, formed by the union of gristly and elastic parts, and is covered by a movable lid, called the epiglottis (ĕp ĭ glŏt′tis). This is open when we breathe, so that the air can enter. When we swallow, the epiglottis closes the entrance to the windpipe, and the food passes across it to the esophagus.

Sometimes, we try to swallow and breathe at the same time; then this little cover does not shut down quickly enough to prevent particles of food or drink from going "the wrong way." The windpipe can not bear this and coughs them out at once, if possible; if not, we are "choked."

VOCAL CORDS.

We speak by means of the air moving strong bands of membrane, called vocal cords, which are at the top of the larynx. The lips, teeth, and other organs, help us in talking.

BRONCHIAL TUBES AND LUNGS.

The lower end of the trachea separates into two branches, one of which is sent to each lung; these branches are the bronchial tubes.

These tubes divide and divide again, as the branch of a tree breaks up into smaller twigs. They end in very small sacs, or cells, into which the air passes.

Get a piece of a lung of an ox from the butcher, and put it into a pail of water.

Its little cells are so filled with air that it floats like cork.

Fig. 19.

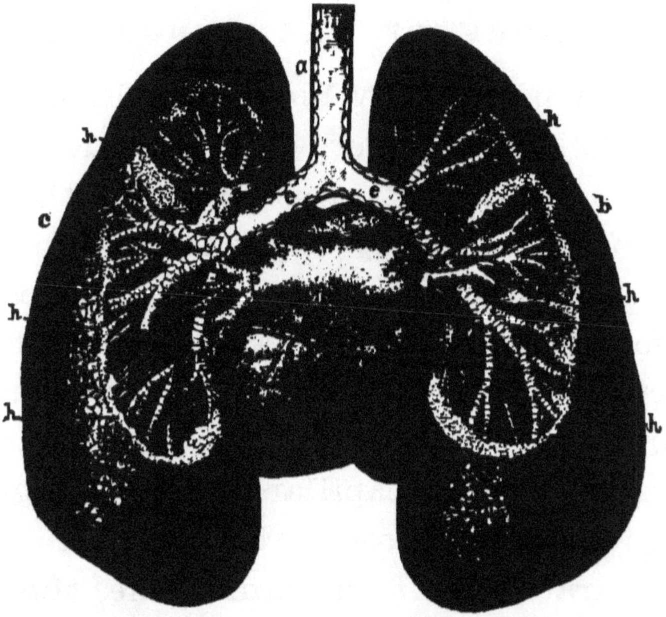

Interweaving of the air-tubes and blood-vessels in the lungs.

a. *Windpipe.*
b, c. *Right and left lung.*
d. *Heart.*
e, e. *Divisions of the great air-tubes going to the right lung and the left lung.*

f, f. *Arteries carrying the blood from the heart to the lungs.*
g, g. *Veins, carrying the blood from the lungs to the heart.*
h, h, h, h. *Air-cells at the terminations of the air-tubes.*

THE CILIA.

On the walls of the bronchial tubes are minute, thread-like bodies, called cilia (çĭl'ĭ å). These move back and forth, and help to prevent dust from entering the lungs with the air, and to carry it out with the mucus (mū′cŭs) when it does get in.

WORK OF THE LUNGS.

A network of tiny blood-vessels, or capillaries (căp′ĭl lā riz) covers the outside of the lung-cells. Having thin walls like the cells, the blood which they carry is brought close to the air in the lungs. By this means, a strange and important change takes place.

Certain waste matters, including carbonic acid and water, pass from the blood through the walls of the capillaries and lung-cells, into the air, and are breathed out at the next expiration. At the same time, the blood takes a part of the air, called oxygen (ŏx′ĭ jĕn), which it needs for its own use.

It is this exchange of impurities for oxygen, that changes the dark, blue blood that was sent to the lungs from one side of the heart, to the bright red blood that is ready to nourish the body, and is returned to the other side of the heart, from which it is sent out by the arteries.

This work goes on all the time, whether we

are awake or asleep, and without our thought. If, in order to breathe, we had to think about it, we should have little time for any thing else; and if we forgot it, and so stopped breathing, we should soon die.

HOW TO BREATHE.

Air should enter the lungs through the nose instead of through the mouth. Even when running, if possible, keep the mouth closed. Fewer impurities will pass into the lungs by so doing, and in cold weather the air is slightly warmed before reaching them, making one less likely to "take cold."

Sometimes, as in running, the heart beats so rapidly that the lungs can not keep up with it and supply air enough for the blood; then we are "out of breath."

HYGIENE OF BREATHING.

As the muscular walls of the chest and abdomen help in the act of breathing, nothing should prevent their free movement.

For this reason, garments worn about the waist, such as corsets and belts, should never

116 RESPIRATION.

be tight. They are sure to do harm by crowding the lungs, thus partly stopping the breath, and by pressing out of place the organs of the abdomen.

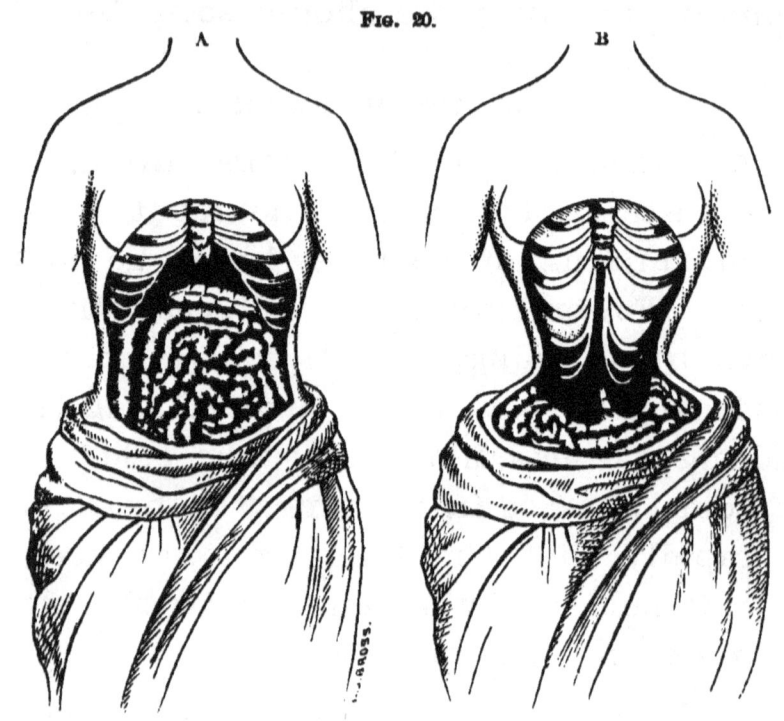

FIG. 20.

A, *the natural position of the internal organs.* B, *when deformed by tight lacing. In this way the liver and the stomach have been forced downward, as seen in the cut.*

Among the many causes of consumption is tight lacing. A small, pinched waist shows that its owner is either ignorant or foolish—perhaps both.

The weight of the clothing should not rest on the hips, pressing the muscles of the abdomen, but be held by shoulder-straps, or by waists kept up by shoulder-straps. Round shoulders, by pressing the lungs out of their proper position, are friends of consumption.

DISEASES.

Bronchitis (brŏn kī′ tĭs) is a disease of the bronchial tubes, pleurisy (plū′ rĭ sў) of the pleura, the soft skin covering the lungs; pneumonia (nū mō′ nĭ å) and consumption affect the lungs themselves, and croup is a disease of the larynx and windpipe.

All these dangers may be largely avoided by wearing sufficient clothing, by being careful not to "take cold," by eating proper food, and by living in houses that are dry, clean, light, well-warmed, and well-aired, and built in healthy places.

VENTILATION.

Ventilation is the removal of impure or poisoned air from buildings and the supplying of fresh air in its place.

CAUSES OF IMPURE AIR.

In a pleasant village, a few years ago, stood a large house, of which people were afraid, because all who tried to live there sickened, and some of them died.

But one day, a stranger looked over the grounds and house, then bought the estate and ordered repairs; when these were finished, his family moved in, and were healthy and happy there.

The secret of the change lay in the owner's knowledge of the laws of health. He provided a supply of pure water for family use, to take the place of that from the old well into which the drainage soaked. Decaying vegetables, old boards, ancient brooms, and other rubbish in various stages of slimy rottenness, were cleared out of the cellar, from which they had been sending poisonous gases through the house.

A long drain was built to carry the dishwater out into the garden; and refuse matter from the table, such as broken bits of meat and skins of fruit and vegetables, was burned in the kitchen range, not thrown out at the back door and left to decay.

The neighbors no longer feared the house, but followed the example of its new owner. Gravel and concrete paths and sidewalks replaced those of decaying boards, and piles of old saw-dust from the sheds went to feed furnace fires.

At last, typhoid fever, diphtheria, and malaria, almost disappeared from that locality, because their causes were so largely removed.

Remember that air which contains decaying animal and vegetable matter, is not fit to breathe; and that water, under the same conditions, is not fit to drink. It is well that winds blow poisonous gases away, that the falling rains wash the air clean, and that plants live on carbonic acid which, in sufficient quantity, is fatal to animal life.

VENTILATION OF BUILDINGS.

Waste matter from the body is always passing off by means of the skin and lungs; fires, whether for lighting or heating, send out carbonic acid; sweeping and the tread of feet set free dust and bits of wool from the carpets.

Unless great pains are taken to keep the air in our houses, school-rooms, halls, and churches, fit for breathing, we poison ourselves.

Janitors of churches, school-rooms, and other public buildings, should never close doors and windows, as soon as an audience has passed out, and shut up the poisoned air to be breathed over again the next time the room is used.

The air in such rooms in cold weather is really carbonic acid gas and other impurities "warmed over." Doors and windows should be opened on opposite sides, until the fresh air has taken the place of that in the room.

No lesson, sermon, lecture, or concert, can be understood or enjoyed by a sleepy, heedless audience—sleepy and heedless because of the poisoned air it has taken into its lungs.

The headache which we so often have in ill-ventilated rooms, is the common result of re-breathing carbonic acid and other impurities. Thus we see that good studying, preaching, and teaching, as well as good health, are dependent on good air.

Special care should be taken in the ventilation of sleeping-rooms. Leave a close room in which you have spent the night, for a brisk walk in the open air—then return to it again.

The air is foul with the heavy, suffocating odor of waste matter, the product of your lungs, which you have been breathing over and over again during your sleeping hours. You felt stupid and tired on waking, because poisoned by your own breath.

Sleeping-rooms should be so ventilated in the winter, as well as in the summer, that the sleeper may have a constant supply of moderately warm, fresh air. This can be done by raising the lower and dropping the upper sash of a window in a warm room.

Cold air is not necessarily pure air, and, in northern climates, is often too severe in winter to be breathed at night by any but the most robust.

Two openings are needed in order to ventilate a room properly—one through which the impure air may pass out, and another by which the pure air may enter.

There are many ways of doing this. One is to open the windows a little, both at the top and bottom, as already suggested. Open fire-places are excellent ventilators. Through them, a stream of air from the room goes up the chimney, and air from without must come in to take its place.

While we must have fresh air to breathe, it is not safe to sit or stand in a draught of air.

AIR IN SICK-ROOMS.

The air of the sick-room should be always pure and fresh. To "take the breath" of another person is, of course, to take the carbonic acid and other waste matter from his lungs into your own. Contagious diseases are often spread in this way.

ALCOHOL AND THE LUNGS.

Alcohol, as you have learned, is sent into the blood as soon as possible. The blood carries a part to the lungs, and thus you may often know from the breath that a person has been drinking.

In passing through them, alcohol injures the delicate air-cells of the lungs. The idea that this narcotic will prevent consumption is a mistake. There is one form of this disease, called alcoholic consumption, which is caused by alcohol.*

The drinker looks well and feels well, till suddenly comes a "dropped stitch," or a pain in the side. Then follow difficulty of breathing and vomiting of blood; then a rapid passage to the grave; for medicine, food, change of air, all prove useless.

---

* Dr. A. B. Palmer says in a recent work, "Science and Practice of Medicine":—"An impression seems to have obtained a footing in this country, that the use of alcohol, even in excessive quantities, tends to prevent consumption.

"The origin of this opinion it is not easy to discover. It was not imported from Europe; for, so far as I have been able to ascertain, it is not held there by any respectable authority. It is not sustained by any authenticated statistics with which I am acquainted.

"Dr. Peacock, one of the oldest and most highly esteemed specialists in lung diseases in London, and Physician to Victoria Park Hospital for Consumptives, when told of the American notion of the preventive power of alcohol in consumption, and asked whether he thought it prevented the disease, replied, that so far from it, it was a fruitful cause of a certain form of the disease."

Dr. Palmer adds, "Too many persons have been made drunkards from the notion that whiskey prevents consumption, to make the view of its bearings upon morals and intemperance a matter of indifference to the conscientious physician."

Alcohol injures muscular power, and, as the diaphragm and the muscles which move the ribs are used in breathing, respiration is often imperfect in those who drink. Sometimes, these muscles are so affected that paralysis or death occurs. Life depends on respiration, and liquors are the enemy of healthy breathing.

REVIEW QUESTIONS.

1. Define respiration, expiration, inspiration.
2. Give the names of the organs of breathing.
3. Describe the trachea;—the larynx;—the epiglottis.
4. What are the organs used in speaking?
5. What are the bronchial tubes?—the cilia?
6. Describe the work of the lungs.
7. How should we breathe?
8. How does tight clothing about the waist injure a person?
9. Name diseases of the organs of breathing.
10. How may these diseases be avoided?
11. What is ventilation?
12. Tell the story of the "haunted house" and its changed condition.
13. How did the neighbors improve their premises?
14. How did the result affect the health of the people?
15. How are air and water often made unfit for use?
16. Why do buildings need ventilation?
17. What is said of the air in churches, school-rooms, etc.?
18. Why does a close room often give one the headache?
19. How should sleeping-rooms be ventilated?
20. Is it safe to "take the breath" of another person? Why?
21. How does alcohol affect the lungs?
22. Describe alcoholic consumption.
23. How is alcohol likely to injure the organs of breathing?

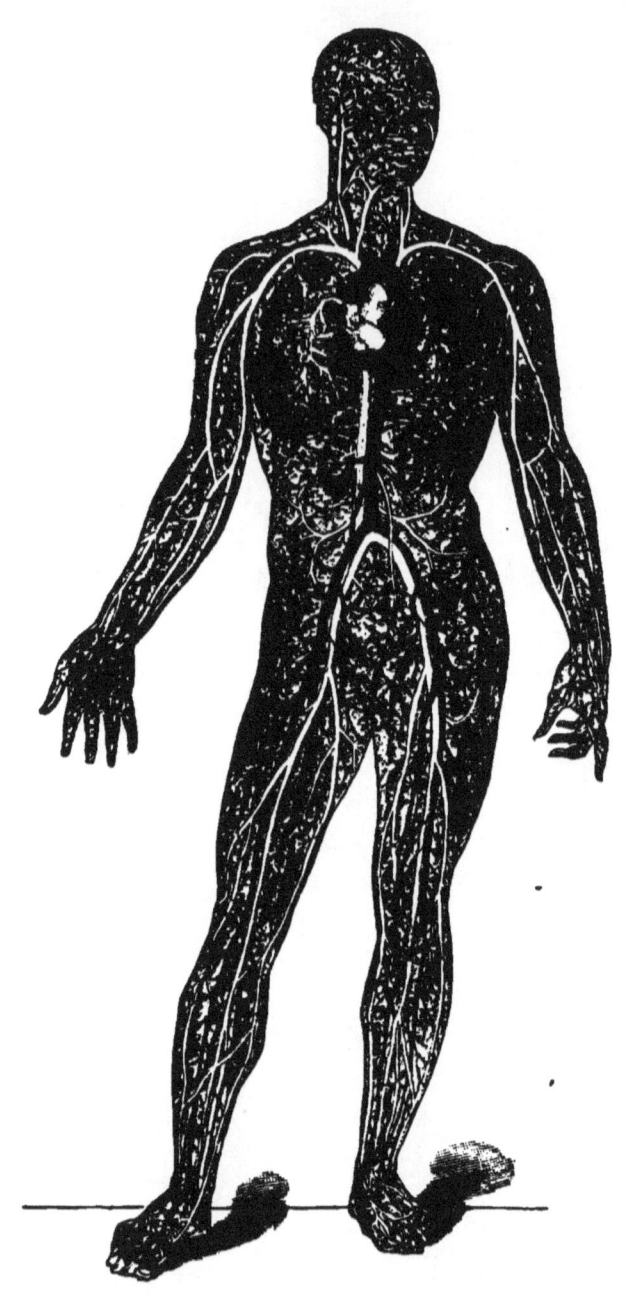

CHAPTER XII.

CIRCULATION.

THE BLOOD.

THE blood is a thin, watery liquid in which float millions of little round blood-disks. As most of these are red, the blood looks red.

FIG. 22.

A, *blood-disks of human blood, highly magnified;* B, *blood-disks in the blood of an animal.*

A French writer says: "You feel quite sure that blood is red, do you not? Well, it is no more red than the water of a stream would be, if you were to fill it with little red fishes.

"Suppose the fishes to be very, very small, as small as a grain of sand, and closely crowded together through the whole depth of the stream, the water would look red, would it not? And this is the way in which the blood looks red. Only observe one thing —a grain of sand is a mountain in comparison with the little red bodies which float in the blood.

"In a single drop of blood, such as might hang on the point of a needle, there are millions of these bodies."

CLOTTING OF THE BLOOD.

This rarely occurs in the living blood inside the vessels. But when blood is taken from the body and allowed to stand awhile, the disks collect so as to form a clot, which floats in the watery liquid.

If the flesh is slightly cut anywhere, and the blood flows—as it will, so numerous are the blood-vessels—a clot soon forms at the mouths of the vessels and stops the flow.

This clot is really a little plug formed by the separation of the parts of the blood.

THE ORGANS OF CIRCULATION

The heart is placed a little to the left of the middle line of the chest. Connected with it is a set of tubes which carry blood to and from all parts of the body.

The little tubes which carry the fresh blood from the heart to every part of the body are called arteries (är′ ter Iz); while those tubes which carry the blood back to the heart* are called veins (vānṣ)

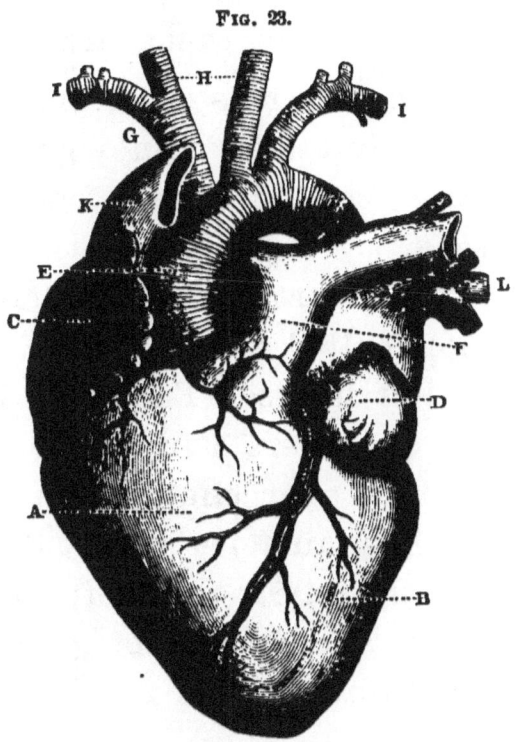

Fig. 23.

The heart. A, *the right ventricle;* B, *the left ventricle;* C, *the right auricle;* D, *the left auricle.*

Connecting the arteries and veins are tubes much too small to be seen by the

---

* The portal vein is an exception to this rule, since it carries blood from the digestive organs to the liver.

naked eye, called capillaries. So very fine are these that the blood-disks have to go through them in single file.

THE HEART.

The heart is a strong, muscular bag, in shape and size somewhat like a very large pear. Around it is a loose bag of connective-tissue.

The heart is divided lengthwise, by a partition called the septum (sĕp′tŭm), into right and left halves. Each half is divided crosswise into chambers which open into each other.

The upper chambers are called the right and left auricles (aw′rĭ els); the lower chambers, the right and left ventricles (vĕn′ trĭ els). As the blood can not pass through the septum, the heart is really a double organ.

MOTIONS OF THE HEART.

The muscular fibers of the heart are so arranged as to contract the two auricles at the same time. The blood is thus sent into the ventricles, which, in their turn, contract together and so send the blood from the heart.

The walls of the auricles are much thinner than those of the ventricles, since they have to send the blood so short a distance, that but little strength is needed.

COURSE OF THE BLOOD.

We may think of the heart as an engine which pumps the blood all through the body.

FIG. 24.

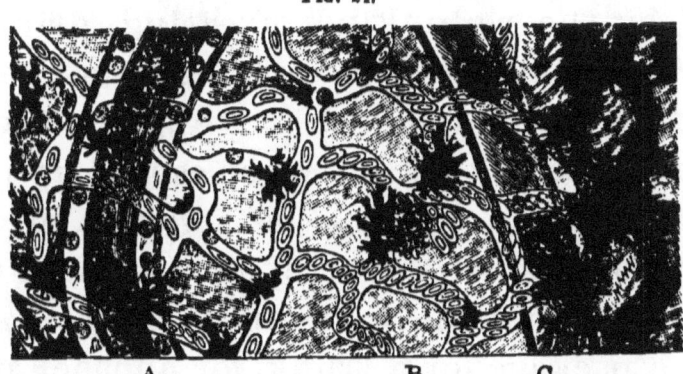

Circulation of the blood in the web of a frog's foot, highly magnified. A, an artery; B, capillaries crowded with disks; C, a deeper vein. The black spots are coloring matter in cells.

The bright, pure blood is pumped out from the left side through a large artery, called the aorta (a ôr′ tả).

An express wagon, you know, carries different kinds of goods. It may have machinery for a mill, a package of money for the bank, a silk dress for your mother, or a bicycle (bī'çў̆ ȇlk̆) for you. The express-man takes each thing to the right place, leaves it there, and then drives away.

So the blood passing from the large artery into the smaller ones, and then into the capillaries, leaves one kind of substance with the bones, another with the muscles, and still another with the skin.

If, by the right kind of eating, drinking, breathing, and other care, we have put proper materials into our blood, it will, in its course through the body, leave what each part needs for its work in keeping us strong and well.

Sometimes, when the express-man leaves a box at a house, he takes away at the same time, a package, or a trunk, for another place. The blood does this, too; but the material which the blood takes away from the different parts, is worn-out or useless matter that must be made over or sent out of the body.

The tiny veins that join the capillaries unite, till at last they form two great veins which bring the blood back to the right auricle of the heart.

By the time it reaches the veins, it carries such a load of waste matter that it is of a dark blue color, as seen in the blood-vessels of the wrist. After eating, newly-digested food forms a part of this venous blood. Sent from the right auricle into the right ventricle, it is then hurried to the lungs.

There the wonderful change takes place which you learned about in studying respiration. The waste matter, largely carbonic acid, is sent off with the breath, and oxygen takes its place. The blood becomes bright scarlet again, and fit to nourish the body.

The veins then carry it to the left auricle and it starts on another journey through the system. It travels so rapidly, as to get back to the heart in less than thirty seconds. From two quarts to a gallon of blood, pass through a man's heart every minute.

The walls of the left ventricle are much thicker and stronger than those of the right, because they have to contract with force enough to send the blood through the body, while the right ventricle sends it only to the lungs.

This, then, is the course of the blood:

Left side of the heart.—Pure, fresh blood comes from the lungs and is sent out to nourish the body.

Right side of the heart.—Impure, blue blood comes from all parts of the body and is sent to the lungs.

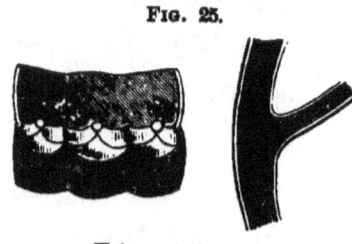

Fig. 25.

Valves of the veins.

This movement of the blood round and round in the body, is called circulation (çĭr cū lā′tion).

Little flaps of delicate skin, called valves, are so placed in the heart and veins, that if the blood tries to move in the wrong direction, the back-flow is prevented by the shutting of the valves across the passage-ways or tubes.

Brisk exercise of any kind makes the blood flow faster, and thus increases the warmth of the body.

The teamster swings his arms and rubs his hands together in cold weather, because his blood, being chilled, is moving slowly, and he must quicken its flow.

The heat one feels after taking brisk exercise, is more natural and more healthful than that which is obtained from nearness to a warm fire.

THE PULSE.

In adults, the blood is sent out from the heart about seventy times a minute; in children, from eighty to ninety times a minute.

Most of the arteries lie deep in the flesh; but, at the wrist and the temple, they are so near the surface that you can feel the pulse, or the motion of the blood as it is sent through the arteries by the "beating" of the heart.

Usually, if the pulse is much faster or slower than the average rate, the person is sick; the doctor counts the pulse of a patient, so as to know how his heart is working.

Rest is as necessary for the heart as for other muscles. To secure it, there is a slight pause between the beats. Brief as each pause is, if all these moments are added together, they make about nine hours of rest during the twenty-four.

WORK OF THE HEART.

At every beat, the heart moves about four ounces of blood.

Suppose you had a machine which could lift very heavy weights. The coal-man brings you a ton of coal, and you put it into a large box, fasten the box to the machine, turn a crank, and the strong arm of your machine swings the box of coal up into the air with perfect ease.

You try a heavier weight—say twenty-five tons; this also is lifted easily, but not so high as before. Try fifty tons and then seventy-five; the heavier the weight of coal, the less will be the height to which your machine will raise it.

At last, you try one hundred twenty-two tons: the machine can lift this heavy load only one foot from the ground; there it stops, for there is not power enough to raise it any higher.

The heart of a full-grown man or woman uses as much power in moving blood for twenty-four hours, as your machine would use in lifting one hundred twenty-two tons, one foot high.

This is what learned men mean when they say: "The daily work of the healthy heart in an adult, is equal to lifting one hundred and twenty-two tons, one foot."

CUTS AND WOUNDS.

The blood in the arteries of the limbs is pure and fresh, and in rapid motion; in the veins, it is impure and moves slowly.

The arteries, being deep set, are not easily injured; but, if bright, red blood comes in jerks from a cut or wound, you may know that one is severed. Send for a surgeon at once, but do something while waiting for him; for there is great danger that the sufferer will bleed to death.

Even a child may save a person's life at such a time, if he knows what to do. The flow of blood must be stopped by pinching the artery, as you would stop the flow of water in a rubber hose.

If possible, take a handkerchief, or a towel, or any convenient bandage, and tie it around the limb close to the wound, and between the wound and the heart. Put a stick into the knot and twist it round and round, just enough to stop the bleeding by pressing the artery.

This will check the rush of blood coming, you remember, from the heart, and enable it to form a clot at the cut end of the tube. Keep the limb raised as you work.

If the blood comes in a slow, steady stream, a vein is injured. The blood in the veins is going to the heart, you know, and is moving much more slowly than that in the arteries. A clot will usually form in the cut veins without the help of a bandage.

If you can not use the bandage, or if this does not stop the bleeding, press a handful of dry earth upon the wound and hold it there until help comes; this is a "remedy that has saved many a life upon the battle-field."

ALCOHOL AND THE BLOOD.

Often the blood is made thin by the enormous quantities of water, or of beer, which are drunk, because of the burning thirst caused by alcohol. In case of a severe wound, the blood, when it is in such a condition, does not readily clot, and there is greater danger of bleeding to death. While alcohol is in the blood, it acts injuriously upon the vitality of the blood-disks, and, when in great excess, may cause them to shrink.

ALCOHOL AND THE BLOOD-VESSELS.

The motion of the heart is controlled by the nerves, about which you will learn in a later lesson. Wherever you find blood-vessels —even the tiniest capillaries—there are nerves entering into their coats and controlling them.

When in a healthy condition, they keep the blood-vessels from stretching or shrinking, so as to hold too much or too little blood.

But, if a person drinks gin, whiskey, wine, cider, or any thing containing alcohol, these nerves are at once deadened by this narcotic; they fail to do their work properly, and therefore the elastic walls of the capillaries stretch, letting in too much blood.

This is often seen in the flushed face, especially in the red, blotched nose, of a drinking man. The unusual amount of blood in the capillaries shows its color through the skin. This is a pitiful sight, especially when we remember that alcohol affects in a similar way, the capillaries of the brain, stomach, and other parts of the body.

ALCOHOL AND THE HEART.

The pendulum regulates the works of a clock, keeping them in motion at the proper rate; remove it, and they "run down," at once. So there are certain nerves which cause the heart to beat, and others which, like the pendulum of a clock, keep it from moving too rapidly.

Alcohol affects the heart, by acting mainly on this last set of nerves which serve as its "brakes." This, like many other of the truths you are learning, has been discovered by experiments on the lower animals and on man.

When these nerves are deadened, the heart beats quicker, but its power is decreased, and the pulsations are too feeble to send out the blood properly. The rapid working shortens its times of rest, and heart disease is often the result.

TOBACCO AND THE HEART.

The effect of tobacco on the heart is much the same as that of alcohol. The beat is quickened, but the power is weakened: severe pain around the heart is a common result of smoking. There is a form of disease of this organ, which the doctors call "tobacco heart."

REVIEW QUESTIONS.

1. Describe the blood.
2. What is said of it by a French writer?
3. What is meant by the clotting of the blood?
4. Name and locate the organs of circulation.
5. Describe the heart;—its motions.
6. State the course of the blood.
7. What does the blood carry to every part of the body?
8. What does it take away?
9. What kind of blood is in the right side of the heart?
10. How is the blood changed in the lungs?
11. What kind of blood is in the left side of the heart?
12. What is meant by circulation?
13. What is the use of the valves in the heart and veins?
14. What is the effect of exercise on the motion of the heart?
15. What is the pulse?
16. How often does it beat in children?—in adults?

CIRCULATION.

17. Why does the doctor count the pulse of a patient?
18. When does the heart rest?
19. Compare the daily work of the heart with that of a lifting-machine.
20. How may you know whether an artery or a vein has been cut?
21. If an artery, how would you stop the flow of blood?—if a vein?
22. In what ways is alcohol likely to injure the blood?
23. What control the motion of the heart and the size of the blood-vessels?
24. How does alcohol affect these nerves?
25. What is the cause of the flushed face of the drinking man?
26. What two classes of nerves act on the heart?
27. How does alcohol affect the heart-beat?
28. How does tobacco affect the heart?

CHAPTER XIII.

THE SKIN.

CUTIS AND CUTICLE.

THE skin has two layers. The lower one is called the cutis (cu′tis), or true skin; the upper one, the cuticle (cu′ti cle). These layers never interfere with muscular motion; for they cover the flesh more nicely than the finest glove fits the hand.

At the lips and nose, this covering changes to a softer and more delicate one, called the mucous membrane (měm′brăn), which extends into the body and forms the lining of most of its organs.

THE CUTIS.

The inner, or true skin, is full of nerves and blood-vessels; it has, also, weak muscular fibers, by means of which the skin is sometimes "puckered" into "goose-pimples," or the hair made to "stand on end."

142   THE SKIN.

On the palm of your hand and the ends of your fingers, you can see little ridges called papillæ (pă pĭl'lē). These contain so many of the tiny nerves by which news is carried to the brain, that our hands are the chief organs of touch. In the absence of other senses, especially that of sight, one learns to rely upon the sense of touch. The blind read by passing their fingers or lips over raised letters.

THE CUTICLE.

We could not bear to touch the nerve-ends directly, for that would give pain in the hands, almost as severe as the toothache.

The cuticle covers the cutis and protects the nerves.

It is made of hard, dry scales and becomes thicker by use, as on the hands of a blacksmith, or on the feet of a barefoot boy. Its scales rub

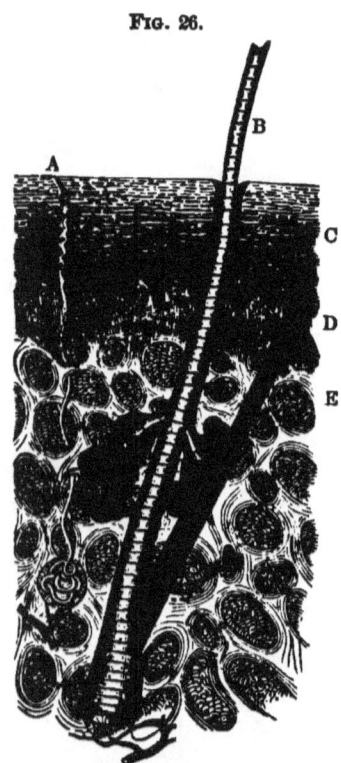

FIG. 26.

A, *a perspiratory tube with its gland;* B, *a hair with a muscle and two oil-glands;* C, *cuticle;* D, *the papillæ;* and E, *fat-cells.*

off on our under-clothing and on the sheets of our beds. In a blister, bloody or watery matter forces itself between the two layers of the skin.

THE PERSPIRATION.

When a workman comes in from the hay-field on a hot August day, his face is covered with drops of water; so is yours after a run, and you say, you are "sweaty."

This sweat, or perspiration, is a part of the waste matter which must be sent out of the body. It oozes through very small holes in the skin, called pores—so small that you can not see them without a magnifying glass. They are the mouths of small tubes that extend through the skin, the lower end of each being coiled into a tiny ball.

They are most numerous in the soles of the feet, the arm-pits, the palms of the hands, and the forehead. If all these drains of the body were straightened out and laid end to end, they would make a line more than three miles long.

Perspiration is at all times passing off

through the pores; but we notice it only when there is enough to form drops. It cools the body, and suddenly to stop perspiring is one of the first symptoms of heat-stroke or sun-stroke.

Mixed with the water of the sweat is waste matter from the body. The skin is thus one of our most important scavengers, and garments which prevent the perspiration from passing away into the air, are not healthful; the feet become damp and cold, if rubber overshoes, which keep in the moisture, are worn for any great length of time.

A little boy was once covered with gold-leaf to represent an angel in a festival. This kept the perspiration from leaving his body, and he died in a few hours.

THE OIL-GLANDS.

The skin is kept smooth and soft by an oily substance sent out from little sacs in the cutis, called oil-glands. A similar oily material moistens and keeps the hair glossy.

The oil, or sebaceous (se bā′ shŭs), glands are quite large on the face, and sometimes the matter in them hardens and dries. When their mouths are open, particles of dirt mingle with the oily matter, and they become dark-colored and are often called "worms." They can then be easily pressed out and the black spots removed.

COMPLEXION.

Small grains of coloring-matter on the lower side of the cuticle, cause the different colors of the skin. When these collect in spots, the skin is freckled.

THE HAIR AND NAILS.

These grow from the cuticle. Each hair has a tiny sac, or fold of skin, at its root. The nails protect the ends of the fingers, and grow rapidly.

You may easily prove this, by making a little mark near the base of one of them, and watching it from day to day.

The nails should always be kept clean and well-cut; not bitten nor broken off. Finger-nails, black with needless dirt under the ends, are not the mark of a gentleman or a lady.

BATHING.

The sweat-tubes will not work properly if dirt is allowed to clog or close the openings. Bathing, therefore, is very necessary to the health of the body.

For most strong, well persons, the best time for a bath is just after rising. The water used may be cold, or slightly warm. If hot water is used, a dash of cold water at the close of the bath, with vigorous rubbing, will prevent the tired feeling that would otherwise follow.

Cold water drives the blood away from the skin for an instant; but it comes back when the surface is briskly rubbed, giving a delightful warmth and glow to the body.

A healthy person need not be at all chilled by a cold bath. Uncover only a small part of the body at a time, and wash rapidly and rub well with a coarse towel. If the bath is thus taken, and each part covered as soon as it is dry and warm, no chill will be felt.

All should bathe at least twice a week, and soap is needed on the whole body at least once a week, to remove the oily matter that has dried upon the skin.

The old idea that it must not be used upon the face is a mere whim. When needed for cleanliness, use it on the face as freely as on any other part of the body.

DISEASES TAKEN BY THE SKIN.

There is danger in using many of the cheap toilet soaps, since they are sometimes made from the fat of diseased animals, and diseases may thus be taken into the system through the pores of the skin.

Soldiers who want to shirk duty, sometimes put a piece of tobacco under each armpit. The poison passing through the pores soon sickens them, and the surgeon sends them to the hospital.

Painters and operatives in lead works, are often made sick by little particles of the lead which they handle, entering the pores and poisoning the blood.

Face-powders, hair-dyes, and eye-washes, do great harm in the same way. Good health is the best cosmetic (cŏs mĕt′ ic). Nothing else will give such a clear complexion, rosy cheeks, and brilliant eyes. Beauty is much more than "skin-deep."

THE SUN.

Sunlight is necessary for the health of the skin, as well as for all the other parts of the body. In many homes, the closed blinds that keep the carpets bright, keep the people who live behind them, faded and pale.

The trees around a house often shade it so heavily that it is dark and damp. Plants growing in cellars have white, sickly leaves; people living in the dark, lose strength of body and mind, as well as color.

The sunlight should not be shut out from rooms occupied by human beings, except in times of extreme heat.

REVIEW QUESTIONS.

1. Name the layers of the skin.
2. What is the mucous membrane?
3. Describe the cutis;—the cuticle.
4. What is perspiration?—How does it reach the surface of the body?
5. What gives the different colors to the skin?
6. From what do the hair and nails grow?
7. How are diseases taken by the skin?

CHAPTER XIV.

ANIMAL HEAT.

USE OF THE THERMOMETER.

THE blood in the healthy human body has an average heat of 98°; that is, if you should put a thermometer (thĕr mŏm′ e tĕr) into it as it rushes through its network of tubes, the mercury would rise as high as it does in the shade on a hot summer day.

This result can not, of course, be arrived at directly; but the blood-vessels come so near the surface that a thermometer held in the mouth or in the arm-pit for a few minutes, will show the temperature within the body. Summer or winter, arctic cold or torrid heat, make but little difference in the internal warmth, so long as one is well.

If there is much change in the heat of the body, it is a sign of danger; in fevers, for instance, the doctor keeps careful watch of the internal heat of the patient's body—if it gets above a certain point, there is no hope of recovery.

But this heat is constantly passing off through the lungs, skin, and other organs. The average amount lost in a day of rest would boil about sixty pounds of ice-water; in a day of work, about eighty pounds. This loss must be balanced by gain.

SOURCES OF HEAT.

The heat of the body results from the many changes constantly going on within it.

The changes which take place in the digestion of food and in the tissues, the beating of the heart, the motion of the blood, the movements of the food-canal, the contracting of the muscles—all the processes of the body, tend to make and preserve its heat.

CLOTHING.

Woolen under-garments should be worn in the winter in northern climates, and many persons require them all the year.

Men who work in very hot places, such

as foundries and engine-rooms, find flannel shirts more comfortable than cotton ones; for they protect from the heat of the fire and do not so readily get wet with perspiration and then allow the body to become chilly.

Loose clothing in several layers is warmer than tight and very thick clothing. The feet and lower limbs of children, in these days of short pants and short dresses, should be clothed with care; thick boots and woolen stockings are necessary for their health and comfort, during more than half the year.

A wise doctor often said to his patients: "Never allow yourselves to feel cold. If you are chilly, put on extra clothing, go to a warmer room, exercise briskly, in some way get warm and keep warm." "Only fools and beggars suffer from the cold; the latter not being able to get sufficient clothes, the others not having the sense to wear them."

Tight clothing chills by checking the circulation. Keeping the body too warm by overheated rooms or too much clothing, is another extreme which should be avoided.

None of the under-garments worn during

the day, should be kept on at night, because waste matter from the perspiration, and scales of the cuticle, have collected upon them; they should be taken off and spread out so as to be thoroughly aired for next day.

Outer clothing removed at night should not be hung in closed closets or wardrobes; there is more or less perspiration on it, and this should have a chance to escape. Be sure that closets and wardrobes are often aired.

In the morning, throw the bed wide open, and, if possible, give the sheets and night-clothes a good sun bath. A wise housewife will not have beds made early; but will let them remain open until noon, or even night.

The family will be gainers in the fresh, sweet sleep taken in beds that have been freed from foul matter by the air and sun. Night-clothes should be hung up exposed to the air when the bed is made, instead of being placed under the pillow.

TAKING COLD.

By exposure to a draught of air when one is heated, by sitting with wet feet or in damp garments, by going into cold air without extra clothing—in these and many other ways, the skin is suddenly chilled. The numberless little pores at once close, and the waste matter can not pass away through them.

It often tries to escape by way of the inner skin—the mucous membrane of the mouth and nose—or by way of the lungs. Then we have a "cold in the head" or "on the lungs," which may lead to more serious trouble if not attended to at once.

One may guard against "taking cold" by bathing the body often, and by rubbing it daily with a flesh-brush or a coarse towel, thus keeping the pores of the skin in good working order.

ALCOHOL AND COLD.

"Bitter cold! must take something to warm me up," cries the driver starting on a long winter ride. So he swallows a glass of whiskey; says, "That's the drink to warm a man;" and drives away. But is he warmer?

Alcohol is a cheat here as elsewhere. The nerves being paralyzed, the capillaries enlarge, and an increased current of blood pours into those of the skin. This makes a glow at the surface of the body, and the man is sure he is warmer, because he feels warmer.

The heat of this warm blood at once passes off from the surface, and soon more than the proper amount of heat has left the body.

Try the thermometer—that is a better test than the feelings; it shows that the body is really colder very soon after the alcohol has entered it. But the deadened nerves can not carry the message, or sense of cold, to the brain, and no effort is made to prevent being chilled, for the man does not know he is cold. This is the first step toward death, and many a drunkard has been frozen to death when too much intoxicated to feel his danger.

When something must be taken to start again the slow moving wheels of life—as, when one is nearly frozen to death—a little red pepper in hot water is an excellent remedy. Clear hot water, hot coffee, or ginger tea, a few drops of ammonia in water, or ammonia (not too strong) held to the nostrils, are also valuable helps in such an emergency.

Arctic explorers have proved that alcohol is worse than useless in helping them bear extreme cold. Dr. McRae says: "The moment that a man had swallowed a drink of spirits, it was certain that his day's work was nearly at an end. . . . . . In that terrific cold, the use of liquor as a beverage, when we had work on hand, was out of the question."

Until lately, the explorer who had gone nearest to the north pole was an Englishman named Adam Ayles. He was proud of being able to say there had never been a drop of alcohol in his body. When in the extreme cold of those regions, he bore the hard work of sledging and hunting much better than the men who used liquor now and then.

Many of those who drank liquor became sick and helpless. When urged to drink liquor, Adam Ayles replied bravely: "No! when a boy, I promised my mother never to touch it; and, if I perish in this ice, I will keep my word." He returned to England alive and well.

When a detachment of the Russian army is about to start on a winter expedition, a corporal goes the rounds to smell the breath of each soldier. Those who have been drinking liquor are sent back to their barracks, since they can not endure the cold march.

ALCOHOL AND HEAT.

Alcohol is no better protection against heat than against cold. Livingstone, the famous African explorer, has proved that men can endure more in tropical climates without it than with it.

REVIEW QUESTIONS.

1. How do doctors use the thermometer in sickness? For what purpose?
2. How does the heat of the body pass away?
3. How is more heat supplied to balance this loss?
4. What is said of woolen under-clothing?
5. How should the feet and legs of children be dressed?
6. What should be done at night with the garments worn during the day?
7. How should sheets and night-clothes be aired?
8. Is alcohol a good preventive of chills?
9. Why does one feel warmer after drinking a glass of whiskey?
10. Is he really warmer or colder? Why?
11. How would you prove this?
12. Name some good remedies for cases of prostration from cold.
13. What do Arctic explorers say of the use of alcohol?
14. What is done in the Russian army?
15. What is said about alcohol and heat?

CHAPTER XV.

ALCOHOL AND LIFE.

INSURANCE.

THOSE who never drink liquor have a prospect of living much longer than those who do. Many diseases are caused by alcohol, and many more are made worse by it.

Of diseases like the cholera and yellow fever, pure air, clean houses and streets, and blood unpoisoned by alcohol and tobacco, are the best preventives.

In 1832, when the cholera was in London, this notice was posted by the city officers: "Spirit-drinkers will be the first victims of the cholera." The poisoned bodies of alcohol-users rarely can resist the disease.

Life insurance companies keep careful records, showing how many years different classes of men will probably live. Here are some of the results of their study in England:

When a total abstainer is

20 years old, he may expect to live 44 years more.
30 "   "   "   "   "   "   "   " 36.5   "   "
40 "   "   "   "   "   "   "   " 28.8   "   "

When a moderate drinker is

20 years old, he may expect to live 15.5 years more.
30 "   "   "   "   "   "   "   " 18.8   "   "
40 "   "   "   "   "   "   "   " 11.6   "   "

From these records, it is plain that those who never drink liquor have the best chance for length of life, as well as for happiness and power to work.

The President of one life insurance company in New England says of beer-drinkers:

"The deaths among them were astounding. Robust health, full muscles, a fair outside, increasing weight, florid faces, then a touch of disease and quick death.

"It was as if the system had been kept fair outside, while within, it was eaten to a shell, and at the first touch there was utter collapse; every fiber was poisoned and weak. . . . . . . Beer-drinking is very deceptive, at first; it is thoroughly destructive, at last."

Some companies will not insure the lives

of liquor-sellers, because they know that they are so often liquor-drinkers.

HEREDITY.

You have learned enough about your body by this time, to understand that when people are sick, it is generally their own fault; either they have not been taught how to care for their bodies, or they are heedless in spite of their knowledge.

But sometimes, one is sick or suffers very much, because of wrong things that his parents or grand-parents did. Does this seem strange? Some one has told you, perhaps, that you have your father's hair and eyes, but that your mouth and chin are like your mother's.

You have heard of children who were quick-tempered, or generous like their parents. Not only property, but faces and character are inherited. Our lives are very closely linked with those of our "blood relations," and evil tendencies, as well as good impulses, descend from them to us.

Over in the poor-house, is a man who does

not know so much as most children four years old. He can not learn to read or write; he is an idiot. And this is because he is the child of drinking parents whose poisoned life blood tainted his own.

Many men and women are insane, because they inherit disordered bodies and minds, caused by the drinking habits of their parents; and the descendants of "moderate drinkers" suffer in this way, as well as those of the drunkard.*

Some men of great self-control may use a moderate amount of alcoholic liquors through a long life, without apparent injury. But their children are likely to inherit a stronger appetite for narcotics and a weaker will with which to control it.

---

* One of the most serious objections to the use of alcoholic liquors in any quantity, is the taste it creates, the habit it establishes — a taste and habit often transmitted from parents to their children — and the very great danger, by continuance in the indulgence, of its resulting in gross, degrading, habitual drunkenness.

Even if a moderate indulgence had no other evil effect, this danger is so great, and the influence of the example on others is so bad, as to cause every wise and good man, woman, or child, to avoid it altogether.

Every body knows it does incalculable harm, and if it does no positive good, there is the best possible reason for "total abstinence."—*Dr. A. B. Palmer.*

HEREDITY. 161

Tobacco and opium produce similar results. This is called the law of heredity* (hē rĕd'ĭ tў). It is one of God's laws, and, like just earthly laws, helps right living and punishes those who disobey it.

The English-speaking races have descended from men who were hard drinkers. Our ancestors, the old Northmen, were famous for their wild feasts, at which they drank immense quantities of mead—a fermented liquor made from honey and milk. In the early

---

* "Three-fourths of the idiots born are the children of intemperate parents."—*Dr. Howe.*

"Where drinking has been strong in both parents, I think it a physical certainty that it will be traced in the children."—*Dr. Anstie.*

"One more example which has come under my own professional observation, may be useful. A gentleman of position, sixty-four years of age, is an hereditary drunkard. So violent is he that his wife and family had to leave him.

"One of his sisters has lost her mind through drinking. When drunk, she has frequently tried to commit suicide by jumping from a window, and by drowning. Her insanity has so suicidal a tendency that she can not be left for a moment alone. She will do any thing for drink—will beg, borrow, or steal, pawn every-thing she can lay her hands on, and even essay robbery with violence in the hope of obtaining money to gratify her morbid craving for alcohol.

"Another sister is also an habitual drunkard, who gets into fits of ungovernable fury when in drink, and is dangerous both to herself and to others.

"The fatal legacy in this case was from both parents. The father shot himself when insane from the use of alcohol, and the mother was a drunkard. The grandfather was also a confirmed inebriate."—*Norman Kerr, M.D.*

days of the English nation, wine and ale were every-where used.

In America, only a few years ago, cider and rum were found in the cellar and on the table of nearly every farmer; and no wedding, funeral, or public gathering of any sort, was without its free liquor.

The ignorance of that time in regard to the origin, nature, and consequences of alcohol, is shown by the fact that the first temperance pledges signed in this country, prohibited the use of liquor "save at weddings and funerals," and the taking of "alcoholic drinks, excepting wine, beer, and cider."

The hardy, outdoor life which was led by so many of our forefathers, prevented them from feeling the full effects of their poisonous beverages.

The English and Americans of to-day are descended from these drinking ancestors, and inherit from them a craving for alcohol, and are safe from the poison only when they let it entirely alone.

The taking of a single glass of liquor, the eating of brandy sauce or wine jelly, may rouse this inherited desire, though its possessor may not have discovered that the taint is in his blood; the appetite, becoming uncontrollable, may bring its owner to a drunkard's grave.

REVIEW QUESTIONS.

1. Why have those who never drink liquor a prospect of living longer than those who do?
2. Name good preventives of such diseases as cholera and yellow fever.
3. What do the records kept by life insurance companies prove in regard to total abstinence?
4. What class of men will insurance companies not insure?
5. If we are sick, whose fault is it usually?
6. By the faults of what other persons may our illness sometimes be caused?
7. What physical traits are often inherited?—what mental traits?
8. How do the habits of drinking men and women affect their descendants?
9. What is this law called?
10. From whom do English-speaking people inherit the taste for alcohol?
11. How were liquors used in America, a few years ago?
12. Why did not our forefathers feel the full effect of the liquor they drank?
13. Is it safe to take "the first glass"?—why?

CHAPTER XIII.

1. What are "goose-pimples"?—papillæ?
2. Is it safe to wear clothing which will prevent perspiration from passing into the air?
3. How are the skin and hair kept smooth and glossy?
4. What is the effect of face-powders and hair-dyes?
5. What is said about the use of soap?
6. Should the sunlight be allowed to enter our dwellings?

7. How should the nails be cared for?
8. Why is bathing important?
9. What is the best time for a bath?
10. Explain the warm glow that is felt after a cold bath and brisk rubbing.

CHAPTER XIV.

1. Is it wise to allow one's self to feel cold?
2. What is meant by taking cold?
3. What is the cause of "a cold in the head," or "on the lungs"?
4. What remedies are useful in case of being chilled through?
5. Should we keep our overcoats, shawls, or furs on when we come into a warm room?—for how long a time?
6. Why is a man under the influence of liquor not apt to feel cold?
7. What was the experience of Adam Ayles in the Arctic regions?

CHAPTER XVI.

THE NERVOUS SYSTEM.

MAN AND OTHER ANIMALS.

MUSCULAR action, digestion, circulation, and all the work of the body, need to be directed and controlled. This wonderful task is given to the nervous system.

Plants have no power to think or feel: cut a tree, and the bark and wood have no sense of pain; the rose is neither glad nor sorry when you take it from the stem—it knows nothing of what is being done.

The simplest forms of animal life have very little of this nervous power; one of them, the hydra (hy′drȧ), may be cut into pieces, and each piece will form a new hydra. But animals which have the sense of feeling —those which can be taught by man—possess most of this power.

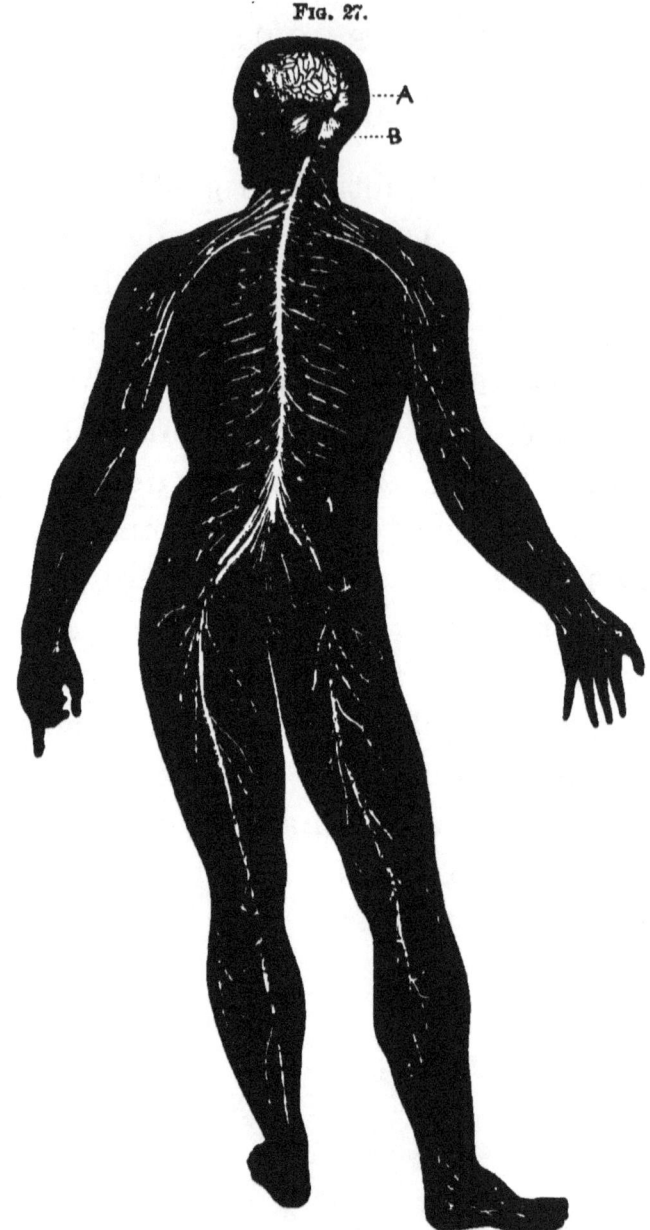

The nervous system. A, cĕr′ĕ brŭm; B, cĕr ĕ bĕl′ lum.

The dog obeys his master's orders; horses are trained to understand the slightest word of command. The elephant, though huge and clumsy, is used in India to build bridges, move and pile heavy logs, and to do many other kinds of work.

But no other animal has so complete a nervous system as man; and so, no other animal can think and plan so well. He is placed at the head of living creatures, not to be a tyrant to torment and destroy others; but to "protect all harmless living creatures," and to treat none with cruelty.

PARTS OF THE NERVOUS SYSTEM.

The nervous system is divided into centers, cords, and nerves.

The most important center is the brain; the principal cord is the spinal cord, which passes down the back through a series of holes in the vertebræ; from the brain and spinal cord, slender white threads, called nerves, extend to all parts of the body. Other nerves start from small centers or knots of nerve-matter, near the backbone.

NERVOUS POWER.

The nerve-centers are mainly composed of soft, gray matter; the spinal cord has a core of this same gray matter, surrounded by white nerve-fibers.

What nervous power is, or how it is made, we do not know; but it begins in the gray matter, and is sent along the white fibers.

The centers are often compared to the stations of a telegraph system where all messages, home and foreign, are received, and whence orders are sent out in every direction. The cords and nerves resemble, in the same way, the wires along which messages are sent.

THE BRAIN.

The brain is protected from injury by the strong bones of the skull, and by three coverings, or coats. The outer coat is very tough; the inner ones are soft and delicate. The two principal parts of the brain are called the cerebrum (çĕr'ĕ brŭm) and cerebellum (çĕr ĕ bĕl'lŭm).

THE CEREBRUM.

The cerebrum is the part of the brain in the upper, middle, and front of the head. It has gray matter on the outside, and white nerve-fibers on the inside.

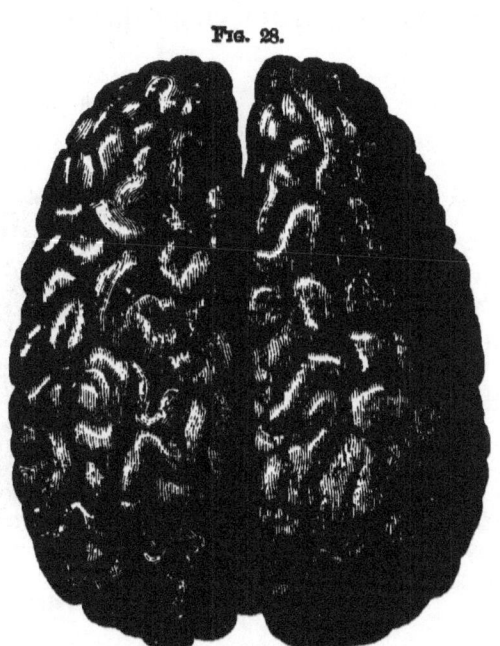
Fig. 28.
Surface of the cer'e brum.

The gray matter is coiled back and forth, so that a great deal is packed away in this part of the skull. You may get a good idea of these wrinkles, or foldings, by looking at a piece of brain coral, or at the meat of an English walnut.

This is the part of the brain by means of which we think; and wise thinking strengthens it, as proper exercise strengthens the muscles. The greater the power and activity of the mind, the more wrinkled and coiled will the gray matter of the cerebrum become.

If this part of the brain is taken away from a pigeon (pĭj'ŭn), it becomes stupid, and takes no notice of things around it.

Fig. 29.

Pigeon from which the cerebrum has been removed.

THE CEREBELLUM.

In the lower, back part of the skull, is the smaller division of the brain called the cerebellum.

Like the cerebrum, the gray matter is on the outside; the white matter, inside; but the coilings of the gray matter are finer, more like layers or foldings; and the white fibers extend into the gray, in such a manner that they look somewhat like the branch of a tree—this is sometimes spoken of as "the tree of life."

Fig. 30.

Pigeon from which the cerebellum has been removed.

The special work of the cerebellum is not fully understood. If it is injured, one can not use his body as he wishes; the messages of motion are not sent correctly, the muscles do not obey his will, and he acts as if intoxicated.

If the cerebellum is taken from pigeons,

they make "uncertain, sprawling movements."

THE SPINAL CORD.

At the very base of the brain, is an important mass of white and gray nerve-matter, situated at the upper end of the spinal cord; it is often called the "vital knot," because one nerve which starts from this center, controls the act of breathing.

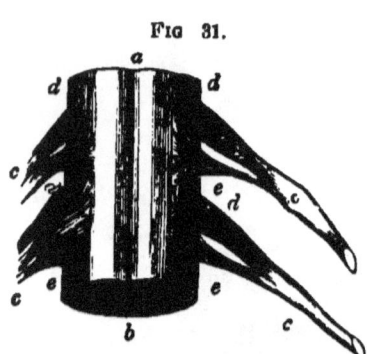

Fig 31.

Section of the Spinal Cord.

a, b. *Section of the cord.*
c, c, c, c. *Spinal nerves.*
d, d, d, d. *Posterior or sensory roots of the spinal nerves.*
e, e, e, e. *Anterior or motory roots of the spinal nerves.*

If the knot is injured near this nerve, as is the case when one's neck is broken, respiration stops and death occurs instantly. This part of the brain is so placed as to be protected as fully as possible, and it is rarely injured except in death by hanging.

The spinal cord, as has been said, extends down the trunk through the backbone. It is a white cord, about as large as the end of a man's little finger; down its whole length, front and back, are two deep furrows.

THE SPINAL NERVES.

Thirty-one pairs of nerves pass off from the sides of the spinal cord, divide and re-divide, and send tiny nerve-threads all over the body. Touch the skin ever so lightly and you feel the touch, because the cutis is full of nerve-ends.

NERVE-TUBES.

Each nerve appears to be a bundle of small fibers; when viewed under a strong microscope, the separate fibers are seen to be really very small tubes.

These nerve-tubes do not branch off from larger nerves as the smaller arteries branch from the larger, but lie side by side, bound together by delicate membranes.

Each tiny nerve-tube is distinct from the others as it passes into the brain. Were it otherwise, we should often be confused and often in danger.

If the nerve-tubes from your first finger

were to unite with those from your thumb, so as to make one large tube, you could not tell, unless you used your eyes, whether you pricked your finger or your thumb.

If the nerve-tubes from the feet united to make one large tube, you could not know by feeling, alone, which foot was cold, cut, or bruised. But when a fly lights on your hand, you do know perfectly well that he is not on your face; the nerves carry word of his presence to the part of the brain which has to do with your hand.

KINDS OF NERVES.

In studying the heart, you learned that two sets of nerves were necessary to its proper "beating." So the lungs, brain, and other organs, are kept at work by certain nerves and held from overaction by other nerves which serve as "brakes."

By other sets of these signal-lines, we know about the world around us. We can not hear with our eyes, nor smell with our ears; for the nerves of sight are affected by light only, those of hearing by sound only.

By the nerves of smell, we perceive different odors; by those of taste, we enjoy food and drink, and dislike some medicines and various disagreeable things; while by those of touch, we are told about the various objects with which we come in contact—as, for example, whether they are hard or soft, rough or smooth.

In the cutis, too, lie the ends of those fibers, or tubes, by means of which we receive our sensations of pain; and there are other nerves which give us the power of muscular motion.

FIBERS OF FEELING AND OF MOTION.

The two sets of nerve-tubes last mentioned, though they look exactly alike, have two kinds of work to do. However closely they may be bound together, each performs its own task and never interferes with that of its neighbor.

One set—the fibers of feeling—carries messages to the brain from the body; another set—the fibers of motion—brings messages from the brain to the muscles.

HOW THE NERVES WORK.

The nerve-fibers are like those telegraph lines on which messages travel in a single direction only: on one wire, all the telegrams are sent to the central office; while on the other, they are received from the central office.

When the finger touches a hot iron, nerve-ends of the fibers of feeling send the message along up the arm into the spinal cord, and thence to the brain, which feels the pain. At once, the brain sends back over the motion-fibers a message to the muscles in the finger, telling them to remove it from the iron.

All this is done in the twinkling of an eye; and the pain, which seems to be in the finger, is really perceived in the brain; and yet the brain itself may be injured severely without suffering, though it is the seat of all pain.

An iron bar was once driven through the upper part of a man's head and he felt no pain.

INJURIES OF THE NERVES.

The fibers of motion and of feeling look exactly alike, as has been said. The large nerve of the arm or leg is formed of many of these fibers bound together. Near the spinal cord, it is divided; all of its motion-fibers come from the front part, all of its feeling-fibers from the back part of the cord.

In time of war, soldiers often cut the telegraph lines leading to the enemy's camp; then no message can be given or sent, till the line is repaired.

In a similar way, if the back part of the spinal cord, just where the nerve goes off to the right foot, is injured, the sense of feeling in the foot is gone.

You may prick it, or burn it, as much as you please; no pain will be felt, because the nerve fiber which should carry the message of trouble to the brain is injured.

If the front part of the spinal cord is injured at the same place, the order to move the foot may start from the brain; but the muscles do not obey, because they do not receive it. The message can not get by the broken place on the line. This is how we know there are two sets of fibers connected with the brain-center.

Fig. 32.

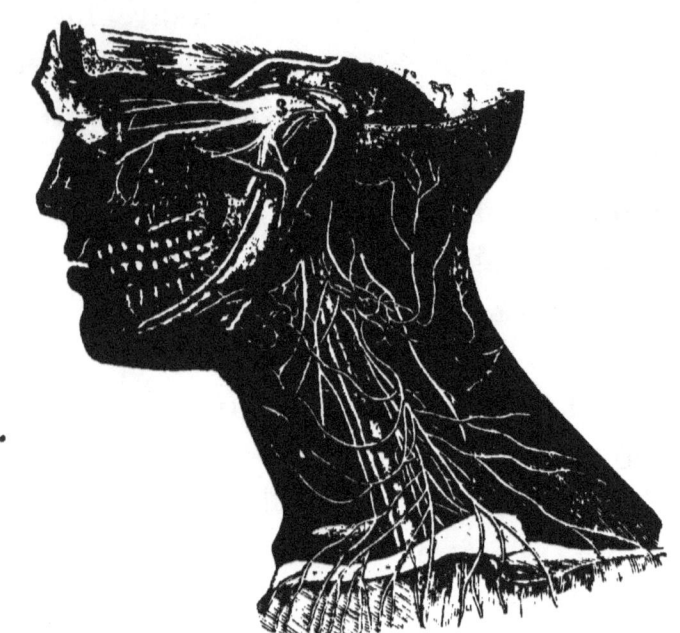

Nerves of the face and neck.

Have you ever had your foot soundly "asleep"? You had held it in such a position that the nerves were pressed, and this partly paralyzed them, so that, for a moment, the foot could scarcely move or feel.

THE CRANIAL NERVES.

If the spinal cord be divided, or seriously diseased or pressed upon, there is no feeling or motion in any part of the body below the point of injury. This is called paralysis (pa-răl′y sĭs), and is quite common.

THE CRANIAL NERVES.

The nerves which start directly from the brain, are called the cranial (cra′nĭ al) nerves.

Among these are the nerves of sight, smell, hearing, and taste; those which move the muscles of the face; and those which control digestion, respiration, and the motions of the heart.

From one of these nerves, a number of little branches go to the center of each tooth, and, in case a tooth decays so that either the food or the air can reach them, we suffer severe pain.

Sometimes, the dentist "kills the nerve" by putting against it creosote (crē′ō sōtе̱), or some other substance. Then he takes out a piece of the little white thread, and fills the cavity with gold, or some other material, to prevent further decay.

THOUGHT.

But the brain has other important work to do besides merely keeping us alive. It is the organ of the mind. By it, we think and reason: how, we do not know; but God has given us this wonderful instrument, and with it we may do either good or evil.

Every time one does right, it is easier for him to keep on doing right, because he strengthens that part of the brain which is used by the good powers of his mind.

Every time he does wrong, he weakens this part, and strengthens the part used by the powers of his mind for evil—making it much easier to do wrong the next time. Thus we form habits that control us.

In this way, boys and girls who are mean and cruel, whose thoughts are impure and lives untrue, make the men and women who do the mischief and sin of the world; while those whose lives are pure and true, make the men and women who are honored and loved.

One reason why it is almost impossible

for a drunkard to reform, is, because alcohol has deadened that part of the brain which he needs to use in order to master his appetite.

The best quality of brain, as in the case of gifted men and women, seems to suffer the most.

HYGIENE OF THE NERVOUS SYSTEM.

Healthy blood is needed in order to have healthy nerves; and proper food, fresh air, and exercise, are necessary to healthy blood.

To keep the mind strong and happy, we must observe the rules of right living, and so protect the brain. When the mind is hard at work, an extra supply of blood is sent to this organ; if it is over-worked, too much blood and energy are thus taken from other parts of the body, which then become weak and feeble. Neither brain-work nor muscle-work must be neglected, for both are important.

Rest must also be given to this busy organ, and quiet, dreamless sleep is the best brain-rest. Sleeplessness is often one of the first signs of insanity, that terrible disease in which the mind loses, more or less, its control over the brain.

Blows on the head are dangerous, and children in their play, as well as older persons, should never give them.

Causes which weaken other parts of the body, weaken the brain as well. Hence, impure air, unwholesome, ill-cooked food, unsuitable clothing, lack of cleanliness — all these tend to injure not only the brain, but the whole nervous system.

The lack of properly prepared food and other unhealthful ways of living, often lead men and women to use alcohol, tobacco, and opium, to deaden their feelings of restless discomfort.

ALCOHOL AND THE NERVOUS SYSTEM.

You have learned how alcohol injures the organs of digestion, so that the food we eat can not make us good blood; and how it unfits the blood for the best use of the body.

About one-fifth of all the blood in the body is in the brain. Through and around the soft gray matter, in and out among the white fibers, are the tiny blood-vessels.

You know, already, that these enlarge from the drinking of alcohol; the blood then sometimes stagnates, and, at other times, rushes through them too violently. No wonder a headache so often follows the glass of liquor.

Sometimes, an artery bursts, because its walls have been weakened by alcohol so that they can not bear the extra strain; the blood flows out, and death occurs at once. This is called apoplexy (ăp′ o plĕx y̆), and may result from other causes than the use of alcohol.

But this is not all. The brain asks for good blood, but it gets injured and unhealthy blood. Of course the brain can not be healthy when made of poor material.

A boy can not whittle well with a broken, rusty knife; a musician can not bring sweet music out of a piano whose strings are not in tune; and the mind can not do good thinking, if it has to work through an unhealthy brain.

A large share of the water in the body is

contained in the brain and the nerves, and alcohol unites with this water, taking it away from the parts where it is needed. More alcohol goes to the brain of the drinking man, than to any other organ except the liver; its effect on the nerve-substance is deadening—paralyzing—as you have learned.

The drinking man may not feel pain from his inflamed stomach, partly because it has but few nerves of feeling, and partly because these are out of order and fail to carry messages correctly. Supposing that the alcohol has been a good friend, he satisfies the craving it has caused, by another dose.

Perhaps he takes it under the name of "Bitters," or "Patent Medicine," ignorant of the fact that most of these are only extracts of herbs mixed with alcohol, and that the harm done by the alcohol more than balances the good gained from the herbs.

When the brain is partly paralyzed by this narcotic, the man does not know what he is doing—his power of thought is deranged, and that of correct thought is gone—he is "crazy with liquor." He believes himself stronger in body and mind; he sometimes talks faster, but thinks less wisely.*

"The word of a drunkard, especially with regard to his drinking habits, can not be trusted. An old, but true, proverb says: 'A drunkard is a liar.' His love of truth seems entirely destroyed. And 'the tendency to

---

* "Among the immediate effects of a few doses of alcohol, are drunkenness, and, in rarer cases, crazy drunkenness and alcoholic convulsions or fits.

"Still further use of the poison, brings on delirium tremens (dē lĭr′ ĭ ŭm trē′ měns), and various maladies of the stomach, liver, kidneys, lungs, and other organs of the body; insanity, and another disease of the nervous system, called dipsomania (dĭp so mā′ nĭ a); the latter is an intense craving for alcoholic or other narcotic substances.

"This uncontrollable desire for liquor does not appear in those who have never used alcoholic drinks; but sometimes, the first indulgence awakens the desire. With others, only a longer use will produce it.

"Most persons, in their earlier indulgence, think themselves capable of controlling their habits, and indulge without apprehension of danger.

"Even when that danger is apparent to others, it may not be to them, until the desire and the habit are too strong, the will too weak, or the indifference to consequences too great for any effectual effort to change this course.

"The longer the indulgence, the stronger the habit, the feebler the resistance, and the greater the indifference—until the victim is swallowed up in his self-invited destruction.

"From this view of the facts, it becomes too obvious to need repeating, that the remedy for drunkenness as a vice, and inebriety as a disease, is abstinence from alcoholic drinks.

"It would be an insult to the intelligence of the reader to say that the remedy for drunkenness is the use of wine or beer, of which alcohol is the essential and active ingredient."—*Prof. Palmer.*

untruthfulness often descends to his children.' "—*Dr. B. W. Richardson.*

Many railroad companies will not employ drinking men as engineers, since they can not trust them to run their engines safely. Many battles have been lost, because the generals in command were so intoxicated that they could not properly order their troops.

If more liquor is taken, the paralyzed nerves can not control the muscles, the man staggers, his hands tremble, and are beyond his proper control. The brain is still more affected, and the drunken talk and actions show too plainly that alcohol has conquered all the better part of the man.

It is fully proved that a large number of crimes for which men are sent to prisons or jails, are committed when they are in this condition.

A noted murderer confessed that never, but once, did he feel any remorse. Then he was about to kill a babe, and the little creature looked up into his face and smiled.

"But," said he, "I drank a large glass of brandy, and then I didn't care."

The poison deadened his nerves and brain, the better part of his mind—his conscience—was thus put to sleep, and the evil of his nature controlled him. Many a man spends the most of his life behind prison bars, for crimes that he would have shrunk from with horror, had he not been drunk when he committed them.

The drinking of a very little alcohol is enough to deaden, to some extent, the noblest powers of a man's mind, and to make him careless about the results of his actions. But anger, cruelty, fierceness—the baser tendencies, in which he is like savages and wild beasts, are not overcome until he is "dead drunk."

Then all signs of life are gone, save breathing and the motions of his heart. Probably the brain of a man who has once been "dead drunk," can never be so strong and perfect as it otherwise would have been.

ALCOHOL AND SLEEP.

The exact cause of sleep is unknown; but we do know that in healthy sleep, the heart beats more slowly than when one is awake; the breathing is less rapid; and less blood is coursing through the brain.

Alcohol interferes with all this, and the sleep caused by its use is not healthy brain-rest, but a heavy stupor from which the drinker wakens tired and often suffering.

A narcotic has no power to cure fatigue— it can only deaden the nerves for a while, and thus prevent one from knowing that he is weary while under its influence.

ALCOHOL AND THE MIND.

No man can explain the connection between body and soul, the brain and the mind. We simply know that a sound mind goes with a sound body, a healthy mind with a healthy brain. Alcohol never helps a healthy body.*

The craving for itself which the poison sets up in the system, tends to the destruction of health, character, friends, happiness,

---

* "Indirectly, alcoholism favors the production of nearly all diseases, by lessening the power of resisting their causes; and it contributes to their fatality, by impairing the ability to tolerate or overcome them."—*Prof. Austin Flint.*

usefulness, mind, and life. The only safe course is never to drink alcohol in any form; or, if the habit is formed, to break it off, at once and forever. The sudden ceasing to drink is not a danger, but the wise way of recovering lost health. Men in state-prisons are not made sick by having their supply of liquor taken entirely away.

TOBACCO AND THE NERVOUS SYSTEM.

Dizziness and partial paralysis are common results of the use of tobacco, especially by the young. The deadening of the nerves explains the "quieting" power of cigars.

When the first effect of the tobacco has passed away, the abused nerves are very likely to tell the user of their discomfort, by leading him to be irritable and unhappy.

What would you think of a young man who, if his father gave him $1,000 to start him in business, should at once burn up $500, and then begin work with the rest?

Just so foolish is the boy who destroys the God-given powers of his mind and body, by the use of tobacco. He is cheating himself, throwing away a large part of the energy and strength which he needs for the work of life.*

It is even worse than this; for often one of the first effects of tobacco and alcohol is to make one ungentlemanly and forgetful of the rights and feelings of others.

Tobacco-users often smoke in the faces of other people, without once thinking of the impoliteness of such an act, or that the odor of the tobacco may make others very sick; the smoker "does not think" or does not care —he is enjoying "a good smoke."

These are not gentlemanly acts, but they are the very habits to which the use of tobacco often tends.

A boy who uses tobacco, must not only pay out much money, but must give up a large share of his health and manhood, in return for its use.

---

* Young men who use tobacco, say: "It does not hurt me." Does not hurt you! Wait and see. In years to come, when you ought to be in your prime, you will be a poor, nervous, irritable, nerve-dried creature. Your hands will tremble, your head will ache, your sleep will be fitful and disturbed, and your stomach out of order.

Sins against the laws of health, not punished at one end of life, are sure to be at the other.—(*Adapted from J. R. Black.*)

In Germany, children under sixteen are forbidden to use it; the same is true of the pupils of the public schools in France; and of the students in the United States Naval Academy at Annapolis, and the Military School at West Point.

Those who run races or engage in rowing matches, are denied alcohol and tobacco while in "training." Each man would be glad to have his opponent drink a single glass of liquor just before the contest, so as to weaken him and make his nerves unsteady.

OPIUM AND THE NERVOUS SYSTEM.

The opium-eater looks old while yet young. It is harder to break off from the use of this drug, than from that of alcohol or tobacco.

In sickness, it often relieves pain temporarily; but when long continued, and always if taken in health, it paralyzes the nerves and throws the telegraph lines of the body out of order, so that no correct message can be given or received, and deranges, often beyond repair, the whole system.

It is a true narcotic. If a certain amount quiets the brain to-day, more must be taken next week to produce the same effect. The opium-user is so enslaved by the poison, that he will lie, or steal, or commit even worse crimes, to obtain the fatal drug.

CHLORAL AND THE NERVOUS SYSTEM.

Chloral is also used to quiet the brain and induce sleep. It, too, must often be increased in dose. Its continued use greatly injures the health, and there is constant danger of taking a fatal overdose.

REVIEW QUESTIONS.

1. What is the work of the nervous system?
2. Name the parts of the nervous system.
3. What is nervous power?—where does it begin?—along what is it sent?
4. Compare centers, cords, and nerves, to telegraph stations and wires.
5. How is the brain protected?
6. What are the parts of the brain called?—describe each part, and its special work.
7. What is the "vital knot?"—where is it?
8. Describe the spinal cord;—the spinal nerves.
9. Do the nerve-tubes unite on their way to the brain?—what is the advantage of this?
10. What is the work of the fibers of feeling?—the fibers of motion? (See other questions on page 202.)

CHAPTER XVII.

SPECIAL SENSES—TASTE.

THE ORGAN OF TASTE.

THE tongue helps in the acts of chewing, swallowing, and speaking; but it is the special organ of taste.

The nerves of taste are mainly in the papillæ of the tongue; as they are covered by a thin skin—the mucous membrane—food must be dissolved so as to pass through this skin before it can be really tasted.

If one eats rapidly, he not only injures his stomach, but loses much of the flavor of the food. When the tongue is coated, as in a fever, the sense of taste is impaired or, sometimes, lost.

The nerves of the front part of the tongue taste sweet and sour things; those of the back part, salt and bitter things. The former are connected with those of the face, so, when you eat something sour, your face is likely to "pucker up." The latter are connected

FIG. 83.

The tongue, showing the three kinds of papillæ—the conical (D), *the whip-like* (h. I), *the entrenched* (H. L); E, F, G, *nerves;* C, *glottis.*

with the nerves of the stomach, hence bitter tastes often make us "sick at the stomach."

SMELL.

THE ORGAN OF SMELL.

The nose is the organ of smell. It is composed of bone and gristle. It is connected with the back part of the mouth, and is lined, like the throat, with the mucous membrane. It is divided into two parts called nostrils.

The nerves of smell enter the nostrils through small openings in the bone at the back of the nose.

The sense of smell helps us to decide what things to eat. If, for instance, the nose were on one side of the mouth, we should not be so likely, as we are now, to smell food before eating it, and should be in much more danger of eating things unfit for food.

When we must swallow something that is not pleasant to the taste, like some kinds of medicine, it is well to shut the eyes and hold the nose; it will not be so disagreeable, if we use the sense of taste alone.

Impure air often warns us of its presence through our sense of smell.

HEARING.

THE ORGAN OF HEARING.

The ear is one of the most difficult parts in the whole body to study or understand. It is divided into the outer, middle, and inner ear.

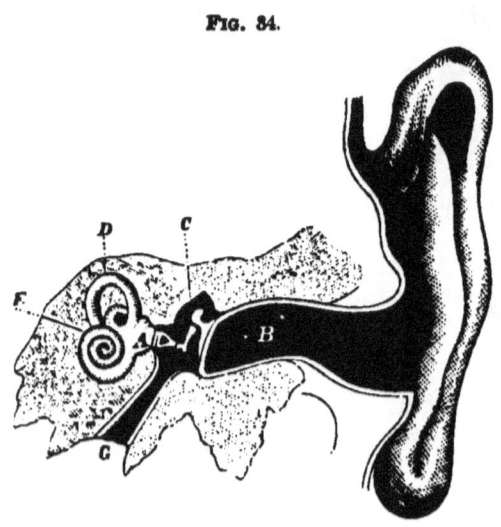

Fig. 34.

The ear.

When we speak of the ears, we usually mean the curiously shaped pieces of gristle on the sides of the head. Their principal use seems to be to help catch the sound.

The opening which passes from these into the head is called the auditory (aụ′dĭ tō rў) canal. This extends to the middle ear, or the "drum" of the ear, as it is sometimes called. The "head" of the "drum" is a delicate membrane which is stretched tightly across the inner end of the auditory canal.

Both the middle and the inner ear (which

lies deeper in the head) are in the solid bone of the skull, and are thus carefully protected from injury.

A tube leads from the middle ear to the throat. Perhaps you have noticed that old people who are a little deaf, open their mouths when they want to hear distinctly. This is to let the sound pass in through this tube, as well as through the auditory canal.

Very small bones, strangely curved tubes, a little water, and millions of tiny nerves of hearing, are found in the middle and in the inner ear.

CARE OF THE EARS.

Very cold water should not be used in the ears, nor should a draught of cold air be allowed to enter them.

No hard substance, like a pin, should be pushed into the canal; for it might break the "head of the drum," and when this happens, the sense of hearing is injured.

If there is too much ear-wax, it will often fall out of itself, in fine scales. It may, however, accumulate and require to be carefully removed. A "box on the ear" should never be given; there is great danger of its making one deaf. Pulling the ears is a cruel and injurious practice.

TOBACCO AND HEARING.

Ringing sounds in the ears and partial deafness sometimes result from the use of tobacco.

SIGHT.

THE ORGAN OF SIGHT.

The eyes are placed in deep, bony sockets in the head, and are protected by the brows and lids.

The eyebrows are projections of skin covered with short, stiff hairs; the eyelids are two flaps, or curtains, of somewhat gristly skin. They have oil and sweat-glands like the rest

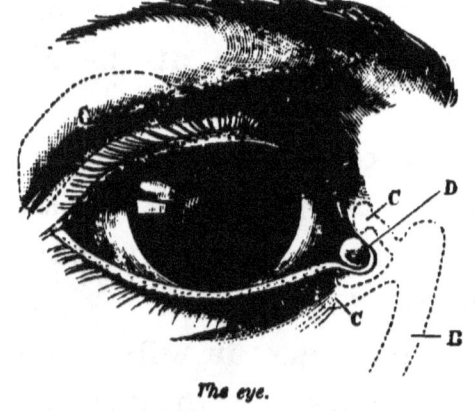

Fig. 35.

The eye.

of the skin, and a row of hairs grows from each edge. These hairs, or eyelashes, help to keep dust out of the eye.

The tears come from a gland that lies above the eye, and just within the outer edge of its roof. Every time you wink, some of this moisture is washed over the eyeball, clearing it of dust. The overflow passes by a small tube, into the nose.

Grief, or even great joy, makes the tears flow so freely that they run down over the cheeks. The eyeball, by means of nerves and muscles, can move inward, outward, upward, and downward.

The "white of the eye" is a hard coat which protects the parts beneath. The colored circle—that which makes us call the eyes black, or blue, or brown—is the iris (I'rĭs). It is like a circular curtain with a hole in the center called the pupil.

When the light is too bright, the pupil contracts; when too dim, it enlarges. This is done by muscular fibers that run round the hole somewhat like the string in a hat-lining; they contract and so draw the sides of the pupil together, or stretch and make it larger.

A cat's eyes can do this better and more quickly than ours. They need to be able to see their prey in the dark, and so can open their pupils very wide.

Back of the iris are various fluids and parts, all of which help us to see. The fine nerves of sight form a delicate expansion or coat, which is the inner lining of the eye.

CARE OF THE EYES.

Looking at a bright light or directly at the sun, dazzles the eyes and may greatly injure them. Weakness of vision and sometimes blindness result from allowing sunlight or an artificial light, to shine directly into an infant's eyes.

Squinting or rolling the eyes, even "for fun," is a dangerous practice, because it strains the muscles which should hold the eyeball in place.

School seats ought not to face the windows, and one should never read or write with strong sunlight falling on book or paper. Reading in the twilight, or on the cars when in motion, strains the eyes.

In reading in the evening, be sure you do not face the artificial light; let the lamp be shaded and the light fall from behind; for writing, the lamp should be behind, and at the left, so that the shadow of the hand will not be in the way of the pen.

A lighted lamp, standing on a white or red cloth, and facing a person, as at the tea table, is very trying to the eyes; the cloth should be of a neutral tint, drab or brown, and the light so placed as to be above the level of the eyes.

Sleeping-rooms should be partly darkened, so that on waking in the morning, the eyes may not be required to meet suddenly a bright light.

Cinders may be removed from the eye, by a little loop of fine thread or hair.

TOBACCO AND SIGHT.

Imperfect sight, and specks of light dancing before the eyes, sometimes result from the use of tobacco.

A certain kind of blindness is caused by this drug, and is cured by stopping its use.

REVIEW QUESTIONS.

1. Where are the nerves of taste?
2. Which of them are connected with the nerves of the stomach? with those of the face?
3. Describe the nose.
4. How does it act as a sentinel?
5. Describe the ear.
6. What care should be taken of the ears?
7. How does tobacco affect the sense of hearing?
8. How is the eye protected?—how kept free from dust?
9. How is the eyeball moved?
10. Describe the eye.
11. Why can a cat see better in the dark than we can?
12. How are the eyes often injured?
13. How should a light be placed for reading or writing?
14. How does tobacco affect the sense of sight?

CHAPTER XVI.

1. Describe the messages sent and received, when the finger touches a hot iron.
2. Where is pain really perceived?
3. What causes your foot to get "asleep"?
4. What is the most important work of the brain?
5. How does one form good habits?—how evil ones?
6. How does the power of habit make it hard for a drunkard to reform?
7. How do unhealthy ways of living lead to the use of narcotics?
8. What is apoplexy?
9. What is the danger in using "Bitters" and "Patent Medicines"?
10. Why does a drunken man stagger?
11. What powers of the mind are first deadened by alcohol?—what powers are the last to yield?
12. Explain the "quieting" power of cigars.
13. Does opium furnish a real cure for pain?

INDEX.

A

	PAGE
Abdomen	96
Absorptive power of the skin	147
Absorption of food	97
Acetous fermentation	23
Air, The	114
Albucasis	30
Alcohol	9
" a Narcotic	12
" a Poison	10
" and Bread	19
" and Cold	153
" and Life	157
" and Sleep	187
" and Water	12
" and Work	83
" Appetite for	13
" Cost of	34
" Discovery of	29
" Effect upon Blood	136
" " Brain	188
" " Circulation	137
" " Digestion	100
" " Heat of body	154
" " Heart	138
" " Kidneys	106
" " Life	157
" " Liver	105
" " Lungs	122
" " Mind	188
" " Muscles	61
" " Nervous System	182
" " Stomach	100

	PAGE
Alcohol not a Food	77
" Origin of	9
" Properties of	9
" Uses of	9
Alimentary Canal	88
Anatomy	52
Ancestors, Our	161
Aorta	129
Apoplexy	183
Arteries	127
Auricles	128
Ayles, Adam	155

B

	PAGE
Bacteria	16
Ball-and-socket joint	56
Barley	18
Bathing	146
Beef	61
Beer	18, 62, 77
Bile	104
Bitters	184
Bleeding	135
Blindness	202
Blood, The	125
Body, Positions of	53
Bones, The	42
" Table of	51, 52
Brakes, The	174
Brain	168
" Exercise of	181
Bread	19

INDEX.

	PAGE
Breast-bone	48
Breathing	109
" Hygiene of	115
Bronchial Tubes	112
Bronchitis	117

C

	PAGE
Canal, Food	88
Capillaries	114, 128, 137
Carbonic acid	10, 20
Cartilage	44
Cavities	50
Cerebellum	170
Cerebrum	169
Chloral	39, 104
" and the Nervous System	192
Chloroform	39
Choking	112
Chyle	98
Chyme	97
Cider	9, 21, 80
Cigarettes	32
Cilia, The	113
Circulation	125-140
Clavicle	51
Clothing	150
Clotting of Blood	126
Coffee	74
Cold, A	117, 152
Collar-bones, The	48, 51
Complexion, The	145
Connective-Tissue	58
Consumption	117, 123
Cooking	74
Contraction, Muscular	58, 61
Cords, Vocal	112
Corns	54
Cosmetics	147
Cranial Nerves	179
Croup	117
Curvature of the Spine	53
Cuticle, The	142

	PAGE
Cutis, The	141

D

	PAGE
Delirium Tremens	185
Diaphragm	50, 109
Digestion	87-108
Diphtheria	119
Distillation	25
Drains	118, 143
Drinking-water	68, 118, 119
Drunkards	14
Dyspepsia	93

E

	PAGE
Ear, The	196
Eating, Rapid	93, 99
Eggs	70
Elbow, The	49
Epiglottis	111
Esophagus	88, 95
Ether	11
Exercise, Brain	181
" Muscular	59, 60
Expansion, Muscular	58
Expiration	109
Eye, The	198

F

	PAGE
Fats, The	70
Fermentation	15
" Acetous	23
" Vinous	16
Fever, Typhoid	119
Food	65
" Absorption of	97
" Cooking of	74
" Definition of	65
" Digestion of	87, 108
" Heat-making	70-72
" Mineral	67-69
" Need of	88
" Tissue-making	69

INDEX.

F (cont.)

	PAGE
Foot, The	49, 52
Frost-bite	154
Fruit	76

G

	PAGE
Gall-bladder	104
Gastric Juice	96
Gin	28
Glands, The Salivary	92
Grains, Alcohol from	18
Gristle	44, 45

H

	PAGE
Hair, The	145
Hair-dyes	147
Hand, The	49, 51
Head	46, 51
Hearing	196
Heart	128
Heat of Body	149-156
Heredity	159
Hinge-joints	56
Hip-bones, The	48
Humerus	48, 51
Hygiene	52
" of the Nervous System	181

I

	PAGE
Inorganic Bodies	41
Inspiration	109
Insurance	157
Intestines, The	97
Iris	199
Iron	69

J

	PAGE
Joints	55
Jellies	23, 44

K

	PAGE
Kidneys	106
Knee-pan	49, 52

L

	PAGE
Lacteals	98
Larynx	111
Lees	17
Liquors, distilled	28
" drugged	28
" fermented	21
Lime	69
Liver	104
Lungs, The	111, 112
" Work of the	114

M

	PAGE
Malt	18
Marrow	44
Mead	161
Meals	99
Milk	73
Mucous Membrane	141
Mumps, The	92
Muscles, The	57
" Involuntary	59
" Voluntary	59
Mummy, The	12

N

	PAGE
Nails, The	145
Narcotic Habit	30
Narcotics	11
Nerves, The	174
Nerve-fibers	175
Nerve-tubes	173
Nervous Power	168
Nervous System	165-192
Nicotine	31
Nose, The	195

O

	PAGE
Œsophagus, see Esophagus.	
Oil-glands, The	144
Oils, The	70

INDEX.

	PAGE
Opium	37; 104
" and the Nervous System	191
Organs	41
" of Digestion	88
Organic bodies	41
Oxygen	114

P

Pancreatic Juice	98
Papillæ	142
Paralysis	179
Patella, The	52
Patent Medicines	184
Pepsin	96, 102
Perspiration, The	143
Phosphorus	69
Physiology	52
Pleurisy	117
Pneumonia	117
Poison	10
Pores	143
Positions of the body	53
Preserves	23, 24
Pulse	133
Pupil	199

R

Radius	48, 51
Respiration	109
" Diseases of	117
Rest	60, 188
Ribs, The	47

S

St. Martin, Alexis	103
Saliva, The	92
Salivary Glands	92
Salt	68
Scapula	51
Secretion, Definition of	89
Senses, The	193
Septum	128
Settlings	17
Shoes	54

	PAGE
Shoulder-blades, The	51
Sight, Sense of	198
Skeleton, The	41
Skin, The	141-148
Skull, The	46
Sleep	187, 188
" by narcotics	188
Smell, Sense of	195
Soothing-syrup	38
Speech, Organs of	112
Spinal cord	172
Spinal nerves	173
Spine, The	47
Spores	16
Starch	9, 18, 71
Sternum	48
Stimulants	81
Stomach	96
Sugar	10, 18, 72
Sunlight	148
Sunstroke	144
Sweat	143

T

Taste, Sense of	193
Tea	74
Tears, The	199
Teeth, The	89
" Care of the	91
Temperature of the Body	149
Tendons	57
Terra alba	72
Thigh-bones, The	49
Thought	180
Throat	95
Tight-lacing	115, 116
Tissues, The	41
Tobacco	31
" and Alcohol	95
" Cost of	34
" Effect on Bones of	55
" " Growth of	33

INDEX.

	PAGE
Tobacco, Effect on Heart	139
" " Mouth	94
" " Nervous System	189
" " Sight	201
" " Stomach	103
Tongue, The	193
Tooth-ache, The	91
Touch, Sense of	142, 175
Trachea	111
Training	191
Trunk, The	46

V

Valves of Heart and Veins	132
Veins	127
Ventilation	117, 119
Ventricles	128
Vertebræ	46
Vinegar	15, 23
Vinous Fermentation	16
Vocal Chords	112

W

Walking	53, 54
Water	67
Windpipe	111
Wine	9, 11
Woolen	151
Wounds	135

Y

Yeast	16

www.ingramcontent.com/pod-product-compliance
Lightning Source LLC
Chambersburg PA
CBHW031815220426
43662CB00007B/651